734.2

D1389940

Items should be returned o~
shown below. Items not alre
borrowers may be renewed
telephone. To renew, please quote the number on the
barcode label. To renew online a PI~
This can be requested at your lo~
Renew online @ www.d~
Fines charged f~
incurred in ~
be charg~

Leal~

Baile Áti
Dubli

THE GREAT IRISH CROSSES

Dedicated to Seán O Boyle,

a dear friend and colleague

Oliver Crilly

THE GREAT IRISH CROSSES

Meaning and Mystery

the columba press

First published in 2013 by
the columba press
55A Spruce Avenue, Stillorgan Industrial Park,
Blackrock, Co. Dublin

Cover by Shaun Gallagher
Origination by The Columba Press
Printed by Scandbook, Sweden

ISBN 978 1 85607 798 9

Originally published in 2010 as *Rún Ardchrosa Éireann*
by *Foilseacháin Ábhair Spioradálta*

Acknowledgements
Cover image of the unfinished cross at Kells, Co. Meath: by permission of the Photographic Unit, National Monuments Service, Department of Arts, Heritage and the Gaeltacht, Dublin; Photo of Crilly family headstone: Ciarán McGuckin, Carnphoto; Drawings by Pauline McGrath OP and Pauline McGoldrick; *Rí na Rún* painting by Paul Crilly;
Photograph of Françoise Henry: Giollamuire Ó Murchú;
Photographs of the Maghera Crucifixion and of the High Crosses: by permission of the Photographic Unit, National Monuments Service, Department of Arts, Heritage and the Gaeltacht, Dublin with special thanks to Tony Roche.
Sincere thanks to *Foilseacháin Ábhair Spioradálta* who published the original version, *Rún Ardchrosa Éireann*.

Contents

Introduction

The great Irish crosses, known as celtic crosses or high crosses, are such an iconic image in the consciousness of Irish people that they can easily be taken for granted. Because they were a popular image in the cultural revival of the nineteenth and twentieth centuries, and because the familiar shape is used up to the present day for headstones in graveyards and cemeteries, recent use obscures the original significance of the crosses.

This little book is a personal journey back to the setting of the crosses in the early Irish Church, and an exploration of the context and the meaning of the crosses and of the elaborate carvings which are found on them. While my own journey of understanding was slow and gradual over many years, I can identify some experiences which quite dramatically moved me from a vague and external awareness of these sculptures to a close and personal appreciation.

Into the workshop

One of these was a visit to Kells, Co. Meath, on a rare sunny day towards the end of July 2002. I spent a good part of the day walking around the old monastic site and standing for long periods in front of the wonderful high crosses, several of them beautifully finished and inspiring. Strangely, it wasn't the perfect crosses which brought me back in time and helped me to view the stone carvings from close-up and from the inside. It was the unfinished cross which became a catalyst for my awakening understanding.

I felt like a time traveller who had walked into the workshop of a master stone carver. A good deal of work had already been done on the unfinished cross. On the shaft of the cross, panels had been carved in relief, ready for the work on the figures which would stand out from the stone. The head of the cross had been shaped, with the horizontal arms and the circle. While the two upper quadrants of the circle were being worked on, the sculptor must have struck a fault line in the stone, because the two parts of the ring and the vertical arm of the cross had broken off. There was chisel work on the remaining arms of the cross, and happily the figure of the crucified Christ was almost complete, raised up in glory on the cross, dressed in the undivided garment, feet heel to heel, toes pointing downwards giving an appearance of upward thrust. The right arm was reaching slightly downward, as if inviting us closer, and the left elbow was slightly bent, hand pointing heavenward. On either side of Christ were the two soldiers with the sponge and the spear, completing the symmetry and confirming the scriptural source as the gospel of John.

Conversation at the Colosseum

It is a truism to say that the crucifixion scenes on the great scripture crosses are based on the passion narrative in the gospel of John, but I hadn't adverted to the significance of that until Pope John Paul II decided to come to Ireland in 1979. I was working with Veritas at the time, and had gone to Rome in August to look for photographs in preparation for the papal visit in September. I stayed at the Irish College. Rome was hot and humid, and staff and students had gone home to Ireland or up to the cool of the hills. The only other person who remained in the Irish College was Fr Michael Mullins, who had just completed a scriptural thesis. After the evening meal, we went for a walk down to the Colosseum. As we walked around the amphitheatre, half blinded by sweat, I asked him about his scripture study. He told me he had been comparing the passion narrative in the gospel of Mark with the passion narrative in the gospel of John. When he described the isolation and suffering of Jesus in the gospel of Mark, I was reminded of the Irish penal crosses. When he spoke of John's passion narrative: Jesus raised up in glory on the cross, the sponge and the spear, the kingship of Christ and the birth of the Church, with the gift of Mary to the beloved disciple, I was reminded of the great Irish scripture crosses – the high crosses, and the crucifixion scene on the stone lintel of the old church of St Lurach at Maghera, near my home in Co. Derry.

The unfinished cross at Kells had taken me on a time journey into a stone carving masterclass. The scriptural appreciation of Fr Michael Mullins inspired me to learn and understand the meaning of the crosses, especially the scriptural inspiration which lies at their heart.

With a Master Stone Carver

I have been blessed in my personal journey of discovery into the great Irish crosses with help from two very relevant sources: on the one hand, I have been guided into an understanding of the scriptural background by Fr Michael Mullins and by the work of Fr Donald Senior and other scripture scholars; on the other hand, I have met some wonderful people of immense skill and dedication in the field of stone carving. In the past four years I have enjoyed an introduction to stone carving at the home of a master stone carver, Paddy Roe. Through Paddy I also had the privilege of meeting the late Domhnall Ó Murchadha, another of Ireland's great stone carvers, and a distinguished academic who dedicated many years of research to the Irish high crosses. The books of Roger Stalley, Peter Harbison and the great Françoise Henry have been wonderfully helpful. However, at the end of the day I make no claim to be an archaeologist or an art historian. This is, for me, a personal pilgrimage, a labour of love.

Oliver Crilly,
Tamlaght O'Crilly, Co. Derry.
Feast of St Lurach, 17 February 2013.

Chapter One

The Christ of Maghera

The unfinished cross at Kells took me on a journey in time and imagination into the world of the early Irish stone carvers. But it was the Maghera Crucifixion which opened the door for me into the meaning and the mystery of the great crosses. I went to Dublin in October 1969 to develop the publications department of the new Catholic Communications Institute under the leadership of Fr Joe Dunn, God rest him. Before that I was teaching in St Patrick's High School, Maghera, Co. Derry, which explains my special interest in the unusual crucifixion image which was carved on the lintel of the old church of St Lurach. I was born and reared about four miles from Maghera in the parish of Lavey, and I was aware of the ancient monastery of St Lurach, of the ruins of the old church, and of the crucifixion scene on the large stone slab above the main doorway inside the tower. However, it was while I was teaching in St Patrick's that I came to know the crucifixion panel better. I was teaching Irish and Religion, and each year I would bring an RE class down to the old church to let them see the Maghera Crucifixion.

At the beginning I couldn't identify or interpret the detail of the carving, though I knew that this was an important and intriguing work of religious art. But year by year, as I talked to the pupils about the sculpture, the style and the figures became familiar to me. You might say that I knew the shape and the patterns of the Maghera Crucifixion off by heart. When Fr Michael Mullins, in the Irish College in Rome in 1979, described to me the crucifixion narrative in the gospel of St John, I recognised the picture that was sculpted on the stone lintel above the doorway of the old church of St Lurach, and that was etched in my own mind and memory.

The Maghera Crucifixion is one of the most remarkable stone monuments that we have from the early Irish Church. It is a sandstone lintel above the doorway of St Lurach's church at the lower end of Maghera, across the road from the present Church of Ireland building. It is a huge block of stone, five feet wide and two feet deep. The icon of Christ crucified is sculpted as a continuous image running across the entire face of the stone. The Maghera sculptor had a much more generous space available to him than the sculptor of a high cross would have had, so that he had greater freedom to elaborate on the details of an iconography which was deeply rooted in spirituality and scripture. Not only has the lintel greater physical scope, but the creative imagination and the sophistication of the stonecraft are so special that we have here a unique work of art, even among the great treasures of that golden age.

The Christ of Maghera

There are references to this crucifixion in a number of significant books on the history of art and the history of the Church in Ireland, but they are scarcely more than references. There is no detailed treatment, although the writers acknowledge that it is a work of special importance. Champneys' *Irish Ecclesiastical Architecture* says: 'It is elaborately and beautifully carved.' Françoise Henry, the pioneering expert on the art of early Christian Ireland, has only a short paragraph in volume III of her comprehensive work. She describes it as 'an elaborate figuration of the crucifixion in low relief'. Fr John R. Walsh describes the lintel in his book, *A History of the Parish of Maghera*. He clearly appreciates the unique importance of the stone carving, but again, the description is short. His very brief reference in the illustrated popular history of the Derry Diocese, *Noble Story*, captures the essence of the Maghera image. He calls it 'an essay in stone on St John's crucifixion narrative'.

The tower of the old church of St Lurach is kept locked, but keys are available from the community centre on the Coleraine Road, Maghera, for those who want to get in to see the stone lintel. The crucifixion scene was carved in a soft sandstone, and some of the detail has been lost as the sandstone crumbled with the passage of time and the effects of rain dripping over the lintel from the leaking roof of the tower. Until comparatively recently it was not possible to make a replica of the Maghera Crucifixion, as any attempt to take a pressing would have damaged the surface of the sandstone. Within the last fifteen years or so, experts from the Ulster Museum have succeeded in making an exact replica, using laser and computer technology. The full-size replica can be duplicated, can be transported without difficulty for exhibition purposes and can be easily photographed.

The date of the sculpture is uncertain. Fr John R. Walsh suggested that the lintel may have already been part of the earlier church which was destroyed in 1135. It would then have been incorporated as the lintel of the new church when it was built. Dr Ann Hamlin, who supervised the conservation work on the church and the tower in the late twentieth century, thought that it may have been associated with the rebuilding which was done when Maghera became the seat of the diocesan bishop. The diocese was then called the diocese of Rathluraigh, now the diocese of Derry. Françoise Henry mentioned a date in the eleventh or twelfth century; looking at the internal evidence of the sculpture itself, it is hard to imagine a date later than the eleventh century. The iconography is totally out of keeping with the twelfth-century crosses. Its theology and ecclesiology are much closer to the great high crosses of the tenth century.

Precise dating would place the work of art in a clear context, but no date would begin to explain the extraordinary achievement of imagination and craftsmanship of the Maghera Crucifixion. A master stone carver was at work, no doubt with an experienced team of stone workers around him, and another team in the background: monks, experts in scripture and theology, living in a faith community which extended from the monastic community into the local community around it. The word *muintir* was used to describe this close community, from the Latin *monasterium*. The word is still used in modern Irish: *muintir na háite*, 'the people of the locality', and *mo mhuintir féin*, 'my own people'. The overtone is of a close family relationship. It makes sense to look for the inspirational context of the Christ of Maghera in the context of the contemporary Church.

I like to use the title *The Christ of Maghera* for the Maghera Crucifixion, on a parallel with that wonderful damaged Russian icon, *The Saviour of Svenigorod*. The Christ of Maghera is damaged too, and it is an icon: an Irish icon, an icon in stone, an icon of Christ the King. I love Henri Nouwen's writings about reading the icons and praying with icons. There is no doubt that we have to work hard, spend time and pray diligently, if we wish to understand an icon, to read an icon, to be in touch with an icon and to benefit from it.

It is worth spending time with the Christ of Maghera. This is a big panel of stone. The figure of Christ stands out in the centre, in deeper relief than the other figures. It is not a realistic representation: the arms of Christ are stretched out on the arms of the cross, longer than human arms normally are. This is consciously done so that the arms of Christ can cover and embrace the other figures, disciples and soldiers. There is another unique feature, which I have never seen on any other Irish cross – perhaps on any cross – Christ is shown seated, like a king on his throne, except that his only throne is the cross itself. The composition is totally conscious: no line or form has happened by accident. And every line combines to draw our eyes to the central dominant figure of Christ himself.

The Maghera Lintel

Compositional Analysis

There are five illustrations, based on a single drawing, with lines erased by Tipp-ex to focus attention on the key lines of composition.

Illustration 1:

The lintel is a single block of sandstone, five feet wide by two feet deep.

Illustration 2:

The main lines of composition run inwards and upwards to the central figure in the composition: Christ seated like a king on a throne, lifted up in glory.

Illustration 3:

Classically, a circle is created at the centre of the composition, which works not just as a physical centre for the picture, but as a symbol of eternity.

Illustration 4:

Within the circle there is a triangle: when it is combined with the circle, it symbolically refers to the three persons of the Trinity in one God.

Illustration 5:

The negative or neutral space under the arms of the cross behind the sponge and the spear plays a significant role in the internal structure of the picture. The sponge and the spear stand out against the neutral background, and that background, like an upside-down triangle, emphasises the cross and Christ the king raised up and presented as the primary subject of the picture.

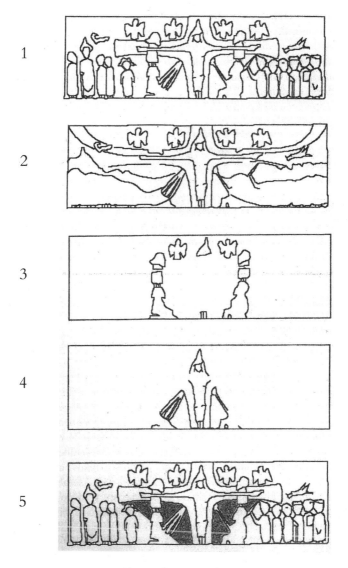

1

2

3

4

5

The Maghera Crucifixion:
Five diagrams showing composition

We should expect conscious, sophisticated creativity from the artists of the early Irish Church. Before he died, Domhnall Ó Murchadha had done a comprehensive study of the design patterns of the great high crosses. He discovered that the measurements and composition of the high crosses were based on regular patterns, and he found an amazing sophistication and creativity in their construction. Domhnall had laid out the detailed results of his research on large panels. They would have made a fascinating exhibition.

When we think of the love of the scriptures in the early Irish monasteries, and how the monks decorated manuscripts like the Book of Kells, it should come as no surprise that the sculptors in those same monasteries should have based their designs on a solid scriptural foundation. Only when the characteristics of the passion narrative in the gospel of St John were explained to me did I begin to look at the Maghera Crucifixion through the lens of the scriptures.

We used to have a tendency to understand the passion story in the gospels as an eye-witness description, as seen by people standing by the roadside along the way of the Cross: a prosaic, realistic description. Modern scripture scholars, like Michael Mullins, have shown us that the different gospels do not give us a cold detached description of events as they happened, but a deep reflection on the truth underlying those events, and on their meaning. The different evangelists give us a different reflection, depending on their own understanding and on the questions which concerned the community for which they were writing. It is not just a description of the death of Christ that we have in the passion story in the various gospels, but a presentation of the understanding of Christ in the community of the Church, of the meaning of his death, and of the effect of these events on his followers, his disciples, the young Church. As a simple example, we might say that we have in Mark, Jesus forsaken; in Matthew, Jesus obedient unto death; in Luke, Jesus the just one; in John, Jesus raised up in glory on the cross.

When we look at the crucifixion in Irish art, we find that it is the vision of St John that predominates in the period before the twelfth century. The emphasis is on Jesus lifted up in glory on the cross, and the birth of the Church flowing from his death. This is true of the stone crosses, but it is also true of metal plaques from the period. On some of the metal plaques Jesus is dressed in the ornate liturgical vestments of a priest.

The passion narrative in St John's gospel is the primary source of inspiration for the Maghera Crucifixion. It is easier to follow St John's passion narrative if we see it, not as a continuous presentation like a moving film or video, but as a series of tableaux. There are five of these tableaux, and they can form a kind of bridge for us from the scriptural text to the stone carving.

Tableau 1: Christ the King
So they took Jesus; and carrying the cross by himself, he went out to what is called The Place of the Skull, which in Hebrew is called Golgotha. There they crucified him, and with him two others, one on either side, with Jesus between them. Pilate also

had an inscription written and put on the cross. It read, 'Jesus of Nazareth, the King of the Jews.' Many of the Jews read this inscription, because the place where Jesus was crucified was near the city; and it was written in Hebrew, in Latin, and in Greek. Then the chief priests of the Jews said to Pilate, 'Do not write, "The King of the Jews," but "This man said, I am King of the Jews."' Pilate answered, 'What I have written, I have written.' (Jn 19:17–22)

The theme of Christ the King is expressed in the Maghera Crucifixion by the size and dominance of the figure of Christ, standing out in high relief from the other figures. But beyond that, Jesus is shown seated like a king on a throne. He is dressed in the long, undivided garment, and the line of the knees can be clearly seen, indicating the sitting position. This is a unique image among all the Irish crosses.

Tableau 2: Unity (Christ as Priest)
When the soldiers had crucified Jesus, they took his clothes and divided them into four parts, one for each soldier. They also took his tunic; now the tunic was seamless, woven in one piece from the top. So they said to one another, 'Let us not tear it, but cast lots for it to see who will get it.' This was to fulfil what the scripture says, 'They divided my clothes among themselves, and for my clothing they cast lots.' And that is what the soldiers did.

On the Maghera lintel, the figure of Jesus is dressed in the long, undivided garment, the symbol of unity. It reminds us of the prayer of Jesus at the Last Supper: 'May they all be one' (Jn 17:21). The whole composition expresses the theme of unity: every line runs inward and upward towards

Christ. At a glance, you might think this was a Last Supper like Leonardo da Vinci's, rather than a crucifixion scene.

Tableau 3: The Relationship of Discipleship
Meanwhile, standing near the cross of Jesus were his mother, and his mother's sister, Mary the wife of Clopas, and Mary Magdalene. When Jesus saw his mother and the disciple whom he loved standing beside her, he said to his mother, 'Woman, here is your son,' Then he said to the disciple, 'Here is your mother.' And from that hour the disciple took her into his own house.

When we read 'the disciple whom he loved', we naturally think of John, the beloved disciple, but the scripture scholars tell us that John left the reference to the beloved disciple open, so that each of us can claim our place as a beloved disciple of Jesus. This short text is used as the gospel reading in the Mass of Mary, Mother of the Church. Pope Paul VI proclaimed that title of Our Lady after the Second Vatican Council in 1965, but the title existed in the Irish language from the eighth century: *Muire, máthair na hEaglaise neamhaí agus talúnda* (Mary, mother of the heavenly and earthly Church). In St John's gospel the relationship of discipleship is emphasised as the most significant for Jesus. In the Maghera Crucifixion, the term is expanded: the sculptor gathers all the disciples (and indeed the soldiers) under the lengthened arms of Jesus, and in doing so creates a wonderful image of the Church.

Tableau 4: The Sponge
After this, when Jesus knew that all was now finished, he said (in order to fulfil the scripture), 'I am thirsty.' A jar full of sour wine was standing there. So they put a sponge full of the wine

on a branch of hyssop and held it to his mouth. When Jesus had received the wine, he said, 'It is finished.' Then he bowed his head and gave up his spirit. (Jn 19:28–30)

The moment of the sponge is the moment of death in the story of the passion according to John. But it is also the moment of the Spirit, like a premonition of the Day of Pentecost. The Greek text says: *Paredoken to pneuma.* The Greek verb *paradidomi* is used when a gift is given, like the Irish *bronnaim.* And the gift Jesus gave was *to pneuma,* the Spirit. The scripture scholar Donald Senior, referring to this passage, says: 'Even the tragedy of death is sacred; the death of Jesus is the beginning of the Church.'

Tableau 5: The Spear
Since it was the day of Preparation, the Jews did not want the bodies left on the cross during the sabbath, especially because that sabbath was a day of great solemnity. So they asked Pilate to have the legs of the crucified men broken and the bodies removed. Then the soldiers came and broke the legs of the first and of the other who had been crucified with him. But when they came to Jesus and saw that he was already dead, they did not break his legs. Instead, one of the soldiers pierced his side with a spear, and at once blood and water came out. (He who saw this has testified so that you also may believe. His testimony is true, and he knows that he tells the truth.) These things occurred so that the scripture might be fulfilled, 'None of his bones shall be broken.' And again another passage of scripture says, 'They will look on the one whom they have pierced.'

The first thing to notice about the Maghera Crucifixion in relation to this tableau is that the spear is clearly visible piercing the side of Christ. Not only is the spear visible, but three lines are shown in the carving: the spear, the water and the blood. In one way, this is the most basic image of the whole composition, because it establishes from the outset that we are dealing with the passion narrative according to John. Why? Simple: there is no reference to the spear in any of the other gospels.

The Maghera artist gives this image a special prominence when he shows the water and the blood as well as the spear. This again is a unique image. It is usual to see the spear on Irish crosses from this period, but I can't recall any other example where the three lines are sculpted: spear, water and blood. There is something rich here: a wealth of reference and symbolism. In the gospel of John water is associated with spiritual life and with the Holy Spirit. Jesus says to Nicodemus: 'No one can enter the kingdom of God without being born of water and Spirit' (Jn 3:5). And Jesus says to the Samaritan woman: 'Those who drink of the water that I will give them will never be thirsty. The water that I will give will become in them a spring of water gushing up to eternal life.' (Jn 4:14). And in chapter 7:

> On the last day of the festival, the great day, while Jesus was standing there, he cried out, 'Let anyone who is thirsty come to me, and let the one who believes in me drink. As the scripture has said, "Out of the believer's heart shall flow rivers of living water." Now he said this about the Spirit, which believers in him were to receive; for as yet there was no Spirit, because Jesus was not yet glorified' (Jn 7:37–39).

Blood is associated with reconciliation and with sacrifice in the writings of John: 'If we walk in the light as he himself is in the light, we have fellowship with one another, and the blood of Jesus his Son cleanses us from all sin' (1 Jn 1:7). Jn 19:37 points us to the prophet Zecharia:

> And I will pour out a spirit of compassion and supplication on the house of David and the inhabitants of Jerusalem, so that, when they look on the one whom they have pierced, they shall mourn for him, as one mourns for an only child … On that day a fountain shall be opened for the house of David and the inhabitants of Jerusalem, to cleanse them from sin and impurity (Zech 12:10; 13:1).

The great writers of the early Church linked Jn 19:34 with the sacraments: the water referring to baptism and the blood to the eucharist: the sources of the life of the Church. One example is the beautiful text from St John Chrysostom which is read in the prayer of the Church on Good Friday:

> 'There came out from his side water and blood.' Dearly beloved, do not pass the secret of this great mystery by without reflection. For I have another interpretation to give you. I said that baptism and the mysteries were symbolised in that blood and water. It is from these two that the holy Church has been born 'by the washing of regeneration and the renewal of the Holy Spirit', by baptism and by the mysteries. Now the symbols of baptism and the mysteries came from his side. It was from his side, then, that Christ formed the Church, as from the side of Adam he formed Eve. That is why in his account of the first man, Moses has the words, 'bone of my bone, and flesh of my flesh', giving us a hint here of the Master's side. For as at the time God took a rib from Adam's side and formed woman, so Christ gave us blood and water from his side and formed the Church. Just as then he took the rib while Adam was in deep sleep, so now he gave the blood and water after his death.

The same understanding is widespread in the writings of the Fathers of the early Church. St Thomas Aquinas mentions it also, and we have it today in the Roman Missal, in the words of the Preface for the Mass of the Sacred Heart:

> For raised up high on the cross,
> he gave himself up for us with a wonderful love
> and poured out blood and water from his pierced side,
> the wellspring of the Church's Sacraments,
> so that, won over to the open heart of the Saviour,
> all might draw water joyfully from the springs of salvation.

I have one other little footnote to add to the tableau of the spear, the water and the blood. St John has a reference in his First Letter which is unintelligible until we make the connection with this image from Jn 19:34. This is the text from 1 Jn 5:6–8:

> This is the one who came by water and blood, Jesus Christ, not with the water only but with the water and the blood. And the Spirit is the one that testifies, for the Spirit is the truth. There are three that testify: the Spirit and the water and the blood, and these three agree.

When we read the passion story according to John, and when we look at the kingly figure of Christ on the Maghera lintel, with spear, water and blood on one side, and the sponge on the other signifying the moment of the giving of the Spirit, the text of 1 Jn 5 becomes clear. The great scripture scholar, Raymond Brown, wrote in his book on St John's letters:

> The logic of the argument is that all Johannine Christians recognise the life-giving powers of the Spirit, of baptism and of the eucharist; and they should reflect that all three

> were already symbolised in the outpouring of the Spirit,
> water and blood on the cross (Jn 19:30–35). *The Epistles
> of John*, p. 599.

I have spent many years looking at the crucifixion scene on
the Maghera lintel, studying it, and talking about it to
anyone who has the patience to listen. After all of that, I
remain convinced that it is a heritage of great value. Even
if it weren't the unique, sophisticated work of art which it
is, it would have a very special importance as a source and
a reference point for the spirituality and the theology on
which it is based. It has a particular value in the area of
ecclesiology, as an expression of how our people in the early
Irish Church understood the Church itself.

The Christ of Maghera embodies a vision of the passion
story, based on the scripture, and specifically on the passion
narrative in the gospel of John. In the story of the passion
as told by John, and in the Maghera Crucifixion, Jesus is
not presented to us as an isolated, abandoned figure. That
is also an inescapable aspect of the crucifixion narrative, and
it receives major emphasis in the gospel of Mark. But in
this Irish icon from Maghera, which is rooted in St John's
passion story, Jesus appears as a regal figure, lifted up in
glory, and living among his people. Here the emphasis is on
the relationship between Jesus and his disciples. This is an
ecclesial crucifixion: it portrays the birth of the Church
from the moment of the death of Christ – a moment which
celebrates his glory and the giving of the Spirit.

The master sculptor of Maghera and his supporting team
of craftsmen had great scope for their skills as they tackled
this big stone. The surface was wide and deep, and they

filled it with rich imagery. Above the arms of Christ are four angels, a spiritual company, placing us in the context of heavenly reality. Christ on the cross is situated like a bridge between this spiritual world and the physical world, between life here and life beyond. The two worlds are also united by the circle that moves through one angel, one thief, a soldier with a spear and a soldier with a sponge, through a second thief and another angel to the head of Christ. The artist, with exceptional courage and confidence, has brought the two thieves from their own space to place them under the arms of Christ for the sake of his symbolic composition.

On Christ's left, outside the outline of the cross, a bird is flying in with something in its mouth: a reference to the dove returning to the Ark to tell Noah that the flood is over – a symbol of salvation from the Old Testament, one of the Help-of-God stories listed in the Stowe Missal and in the Martyrology of Oengus from the year AD 800. On the other side of the cross, on Christ's right, there is what remains of a little animal. The soft sandstone has crumbled, and it is impossible to make out the detail. I once was shown a photograph taken in 1955, and it was slightly clearer. It looked like a sheep or lamb, facing away from the cross, but with its head turned back towards the cross, like the lamb on the head of the scripture cross in Durrow. I thought of the paschal lamb, but then concluded that it might possibly be the sheep of Abraham's sacrifice, another of the Help-of-God stories from the Old Testament, which appears on at least twelve of the great high crosses – another symbol of salvation.

The Maghera Crucifixion is marked by discipline and by sophistication: there is strength and energy in the lines and shapes, and in the way each figure defines a place for the figures near it. The lines and forms work together to emphasise the central importance of the figure of Christ, sitting as a king on a throne among his disciples. As we contemplate this remarkable sculpture, we can find a place here for ourselves in the presence of the heavenly and earthly Church. Surely that's how it was before the later tower obscured the doorway? As people approached and passed under the imposing lintel to enter the church for Mass, they themselves would for a moment have become an extension of the image, and been gathered into the company of the apostles.

Rí na Rún 'The King of the Mysteries'

Chapter Two

The Road to Carndonagh
The early crosses of the 7th and 8th centuries

Two hugely significant events in my life happened in 1979: my mother died, God rest her, and Pope John Paul II came to Ireland. I was working in the Catholic Communications Institute at the time, and the papal visit had a major impact on our work. Part of that work took me to Rome in August of 1979, and it was while staying in the Irish College that I met Fr Michael Mullins and got a whole new perspective on the iconography of the early Irish crosses and their rich scriptural inspiration.

I was friendly with Paddy and Monica Roe, a wonderful couple who lived in the Dublin mountains near where I was living at the time at the Stillorgan end of Booterstown Avenue. Shortly after my mother's death, I went up to visit Paddy and Monica. Paddy is a master stone carver, and the family business was based in a granite quarry in Barr na Coille. They quarried and worked stone for massive altars and other church furnishings, for restoration work on famous public buildings, and for gravestones. I asked Paddy if there was any way I could get a headstone for my mother's grave that would take its inspiration from the Maghera Crucifixion. Paddy asked a question which I have since heard frequently from a wide variety of people: 'What's the Maghera Crucifixion?' I took out a little card and drew a rough sketch. 'Leave that with me', said Paddy. I thought he was going to ask one of the stone workers at the quarry to shape a rough replica of the cross. Instead, he asked Domhnall Ó Murchadha, one of the great stone carvers, to make the headstone. Domhnall taught the skills of stone carving, with Paddy Roe, in the National College of Art and Design, and he and his wife Máirín were close friends and colleagues of Françoise Henry in UCD.

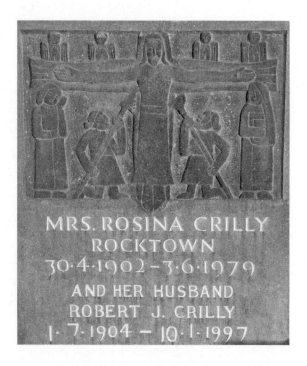

Crilly Headstone by Domhnall Ó Murchadha

Domhnall designed and carved my mother's headstone on a grey limestone slab. The stone wasn't wide enough to take the full shape of the Maghera Crucifixion, but Domhnall carved an original work with the same inspiration: the four angels, the strong regal figure of Christ in the undivided garment, long arms stretched out, the two soldiers with the sponge and the spear, Mary, Mother of the heavenly and earthly Church on one side and John the Evangelist on the other, under the protecting arms of Jesus. I met Domhnall because of the headstone, and was invited to visit him, his wife Máirín and their son Giollamuire in their north Dublin home. It was a great privilege to hear him talk of his research into the high crosses.

The hyssop stick with the sponge, and the spear on the other side, create a symmetrical triangle with the head of Christ at the top. This triangular motif is a central feature of most of the great crosses from the late seventh century until the tenth, and even into the eleventh, if that's where we place the Maghera lintel. It is a scripture-based motif, and one which confirms that we are dealing with the passion story from the gospel of John. The other gospels have the reference to the sponge, but the spear is unique to John. Some writers have expressed surprise that the spear and the sponge should appear together in the same picture. They were clearly expecting a realistic representation, and they would say that the sponge was offered to Jesus before his death, while he was pierced by the spear after he had died. There is no real difficulty, of course, because the artists are approaching their work from a very different perspective. They are not concerned with the sequence of events in 'real time', but with symbolic meaning and symmetrical design.

The triangular motif of sponge and spear appears in various representations of the crucifixion outside of Ireland. Comparison is sometimes made with a Syrian image from the Codex Rabula (AD 586), and with a ninth-century fresco which was in the church of Saints John and Paul near the Irish College in Rome. Christians were reluctant to use the image of the crucifixion in art in the early centuries: it was too close, too painful and too scandalous, but when they began to make images of the crucifixion, they often depicted Christ raised up in glory on the cross, surrounded by his disciples. There is a seal from the fourth century which shows Christ with lengthened arms and six apostle figures gathered under each arm.

The earliest Irish crosses have simple line drawings, representing the shape of the cross, but without the figure of Christ. Sometimes the lines were elaborated into ribbons, and perhaps surrounded by geometrical decoration. But it was a large step from lines drawn on the surface of the stone to creating the shape of the cross in the stone.

Fahan and Carndonagh
This little book is not a thesis or a work of academic research. What I have come to know about the Irish crosses is the result of a personal pilgrimage, with input from friendly scripture scholars and stone workers. My pilgrimage begins in Maghera in the diocese of Derry, roughly in the eleventh century, at the old church of St Lurach. I am going to stay in the diocese of Derry now, but to go back to the end of the seventh and the beginning of the eighth century.

Fahan Cross-slab

There is a stone slab on the site of the ancient monastery at
Fahan in Inishowen, on the main road between Derry and
Buncrana. Although this 'cross' is still in the shape of a slab,
it is about nine feet high, and there are little projections on
either side, as if the sculptor was trying to indicate the
beginnings of the form of a cross. It is sometimes suggested
that additional pieces of stone may have been attached to
these projections to make the cross shape more significant,
but that these pieces had broken off and were lost.

On the front and back of the cross slab, cross shapes have
been intricately carved in the form of broad interlacing
ribbons. There are human figures also, and a Greek
inscription: 'Glory and honour to the Father and to the Son
and to the Holy Spirit', a formula used at the Council of
Toledo in the year AD 633, presided over by Isidore of
Seville. St Mura's monastery in Fahan was of some
importance in the seventh century. It was connected with
Derry and Iona, and St Mura was a patron of the main
branch of the northern Uí Néill, whose power base was at
Aileach, not far from Fahan.

Without leaving Inishowen, the next stop on my
pilgrimage takes me over to Carndonagh. There is a very
unusual cross just outside the town, near the Church of
Ireland church, as the road makes a sharp right turn towards
Ballyliffin. Françoise Henry believed that it was the same
sculptor who made the Fahan cross slab who created the
Carndonagh cross. If that is the case, and it seems very likely,
then the artist who struggled to create the beginnings of a
cross shape from the Fahan slab has succeeded in
Carndonagh beyond all expectation. He has created from

The Carndonagh Cross

the hard stone a well-defined cross, whose lines are softly organic like a free-hand drawing.

As we approach from Carndonagh, we see the east face of the cross. There is an interlaced cross of broad ribbons at the top, and Christ in glory on the shaft of the cross with his right hand raised in blessing. There are figures beside him, three figures under his feet, and a line of figures going up the narrow side of the cross. The cross is really beautiful. I am inclined to believe that we have here a version of the passion story of St John – the two soldiers on either side of Jesus, without the sponge or the spear being shown, and the apostles going across the bottom and up the side, indicating the birth of the Church. Of course, there's no way to prove that, and the professional scholars couldn't bet their academic reputation on it, but I'll go with my instinct! There is no doubt that Carndonagh stands at the beginning of a procession of high crosses which will lead us to places like Ardboe, Donaghmore, Armagh, Kells, Monasterboice, Clonmacnois and Durrow. And while it is not a ringed cross, it is certainly high! Françoise Henry wrote:

> The Carndonagh cross, which stands a few miles further north from Fahan, and is obviously a product of the same workshop, marks the final victory in the attempt to free the cross from the slab. It is cut from a thin slab of sandstone, its contours sinuous and slightly irregular, drawn by a man who shrank from the use of straight lines, and stands a little more than ten feet high. One side is completely covered by a close weaving of broad ribbons. On the other, patterns and figures, sharply engraved, form a continuous ornament, ever on the same level of the stone. The whole composition is organized around the oval of a head, emphatically stressed, that of Christ in glory,

surrounded by four simplified figures, which, like the
figures on the Fahan slab, are shown without arms. Above
is a large cross of ribbons; below, three figures in profile.
(*Irish Art in the Early Christian Period*, Cornell University
Press, vol. I, p. 128.)

There is another interesting cross in Inishowen: the Clonca
cross. We often find crosses in groups in different parts of
the country. Niall Ó Dónaill has a beautiful description in
his book, *Na Glúnta Rosannacha*, of the way the dwelling
houses are scattered over the coast of the Rosses. 'The houses
had settled like flocks of birds beside the sea', he said, like
the seagulls and other seabirds flying in and coming to land
wherever the wind guided them. The great crosses of
Ireland flock here and there over the countryside: there are
nests of them, in the north in Inishowen, in Armagh,
Donaghmore, Ardboe, Drumcliff; in the midlands in
Clonmacnois and Durrow; in the east in Monasterboice
and Kells, in Moone and Castledermot; and in Kilkenny
and Tipperary (Ahenny). Strangely, before the twelfth
century there are no examples of the great figured crosses
to be found in the west or in the southwest.

Location

The great scripture crosses from the late seventh until the
tenth and into the eleventh centuries are found on monastic
sites. These stone crosses are extraordinary works of art. It
is not easy to explain how they came to be created, or how
they were carved with such a perfect finish, given the
limitations of the tools available at the time. It seems clear
that they grew out of the strength and spiritual energy of
the living faith of the monasteries, from the upward and

outward surge of the Spirit which not only affected the life of the Church in Ireland, but which took the great missionaries all over Europe, which left us the Book of Kells and the Ardagh Chalice and a heritage which inspires artists and musicians to this day.

The high crosses are very beautiful, but they were not used in the monasteries for decoration. Neither were they elaborate headstones to mark the graves of the mighty. They played their part in the daily spiritual and liturgical life of the monasteries themselves. Crosses placed around the monastic boundaries marked the lands as sacred space. If there was an inner line of crosses, they marked an even more sacred space, not unlike the significance of the standing stones around the burial place of Newgrange in pre-Christian times. There is a map of a monastery in the Book of Moling which marks the positions of a variety of crosses. As well as boundary crosses, there would be a major cross, like the Cross of the Scriptures in Clonmacnois, with an important liturgical role.

At the hours of prayer, a bell would be rung. The monks and the local people would gather at the cross. Prayers would be said in front of the cross and then at the other side of it. There are references to the face of the cross and the back of the cross. The crosses were also linked with prayer outside of the liturgy, like Greek or Russian icons. They would inspire devotion and provide a foundation for spiritual contemplation. They would support teaching, of course, but it is not true to say that their main function was to be visual aids for religious education. The great Irish religious artist Patrick Pye in our own day has written, in the introduction to his wonderful book of etchings, *Apples and Angels*: 'Art does not tell us what to believe; it tells us what it feels like to believe.'

We are dealing with stone crosses, but it seems clear that there were other crosses in existence: wooden crosses, or metal crosses, or wooden crosses encased in metal. The influence of metal construction can be discerned on the stone crosses of Ahenny in Co. Tipperary, for example. The reinforcement of wooden crosses may be a part explanation for the circle around the head of the Irish high crosses. But it is generally agreed that there is a deeper meaning to it. Some people see it as linked with the circle of the sun – Christ, the true sun, replacing the worship of the sun in pre-Christian times. When the figure of Christ is in the centre of the circle, it is easy to see the symbolism of Christ at the centre of all creation. Roger Stalley suggests that the ring of the cross may refer to the victory wreath:

> The idea of a cross in a circle had a long history before it reached Ireland. In the fourth and fifth centuries AD the motif was already being used by the Romans on carved ivories and sculptured sarcophagi. The circle was usually designed as a wreath, an ancient symbol of triumph, to underline the fact that Christ's suffering on the cross led to victory over death. Sometimes the wreath consisted of fruit and flowers, representing rebirth and renewal. In these early designs it was normal for the cross to be completely enclosed within the circular frame, but a linen hanging from Egypt (*c.*AD 500) shows an arrangement that foreshadows the design of the Irish crosses. (*Textile from Coptic Egypt, Minneapolis Institute of Arts.*) The ringed cross was thus a symbolic form known to the early Christians and familiar to the Irish monks. (Stalley: *Irish High Crosses*, p. 9.)

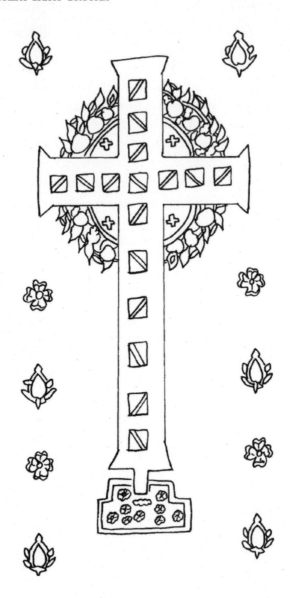

Linen hanging from Egypt, c.AD 500.

This is not an isolated example of the influence of the Egyptian monasteries being felt in Ireland.

Sandstone was often used in the construction of the high crosses. Sandstone is used in the crosses of Ardboe, Armagh, Drumcliff, Fahan, Carndonagh, Kells, Monasterboice and Clonmacnois, for example. The quality of the stone varies from place to place, and when the material used was a soft sandstone, as in Ardboe, exposure to the weather damaged the surface of the stone and the detail of the carving over the years. The lintel of the old church in Maghera, Co. Derry, is of sandstone also, and some details of the sculpture have crumbled with age and damp. The crosses of Monasterboice and Clonmacnois were made of a harder sandstone, with a greater quartz content, and the sculptures are generally in good condition still. Nevertheless, the Cross of the Scriptures in Clonmacnois and a number of others have been taken indoors for better protection and display. A full-size replica has been placed outside in the original location. The crosses at Moone and Castledermot are made of granite. It is a hard, long-lasting material, and harder to work. It is interesting to notice the differences that result in the style of carving.

Inspiration
The crosses display extraordinary craftsmanship, whatever the material. Whether the carving is based on geometrical decoration such as interlaced ribbons, or involves animal or human forms, there is imaginative creativity, and the highest level of technical skill and finished workmanship. This is true also of the quality of the crosses found in

different locations. Crosses at Ahenny and Castledermot, sculpted around the same time, differ in style, not because of variations in skill, but because of the nature of the stone that was available locally, and because of the vision that inspired the stone workers. Over the years, skill and experience grew, and inspiration focused more and more on figurative sculpture rooted in theology and scripture.

The process begins with the inspiration. The Donegal writer, Seosamh Mac Grianna, said of his fellow author Pádraic Ó Conaire: 'He found the words and the images that were necessary to express deep thought with clarity' (*Pádraig Ó Conaire agus Aistí Eile*, p. 27). Mac Grianna praised Ó Conaire's choice of words and images, but the process began with the deep thought. Similarly with the artists who created the great stone crosses: their creativity and their craftsmanship were miraculous, but they were at the service of the vision which inspired them. Françoise Henry wrote:

> Before coming to the description of the chief crosses, we shall have to examine the themes directing the organization of the picture sequences which cover them, as the scenes are not chosen in a haphazard way, but for the inner meaning of the episode represented. They have not been carved merely to depict an event, but to show it as foreshadowing another event or as illustrating a theological idea. In this respect they fit perfectly into the representational pattern of paleo-Christian and Romanesque art. They are the pictorial form of a thought, before being a composition of figures in a frame. This does not necessarily mean that composition is considered as unimportant or negligible. Still it is essential to note from the start that the idea is the dominant factor and very often

explains the composition or some of its features. (*Irish Art During the Viking Invasions*, pp 140–41)

The most basic inspiration which underpins the great stone crosses of Ireland is the sacred scripture, Old Testament and New Testament. Françoise Henry, and later Peter Harbison, did extraordinary work in interpreting and explaining the images on the high crosses, including the many images based on Old Testament stories. But there isn't a great deal of detailed analysis of the most central image of all: the image of Christ crucified. Perhaps that is understandable. Once the image was identified as '*the crucifixion*', scholars might naturally turn their attention to the panels which were obscure or difficult to interpret. They focused their concentration and their research on those, and indeed with outstanding results. Because of their efforts, we can all learn to appreciate the themes which flow through our pre-Norman sculptural heritage.

It is important to focus a great deal of concentration on the image of the crucifixion as we find it on our great crosses. For a long time we tended to look at the crosses and accept the image of the crucifixion simply as '*the crucifixion*'. We had recognised it, and there was no need to go any further. But in recent years scripture scholars have been demonstrating that there are great differences between the presentations of the crucifixion in the different gospels. The passion story in Mark is not the same as the passion story in John, for example. Consequently, when we look at the representation of the crucifixion in a work of art, we need to ask: what is the emphasis in this crucifixion scene? Is it inspired by the gospel of Mark, of Matthew, of Luke, of John?

I discovered a new understanding of the Maghera Crucifixion in August 1979, when Fr Michael Mullins drew my attention to the context of the passion narrative in St John's gospel. I'm sure Fr Wilfrid Harrington, who taught me scripture in Maynooth, would have been very disappointed with me, but I hadn't really taken note of the fact that the spear piercing the side of Christ was a pointer to the gospel of John. (It is now the basis for my presentation on 'How to bluff your way in early Irish art!') Once I realised that the Maghera Crucifixion showed Jesus raised up in glory, and the birth of the Church – emphasised by the sponge and the spear and the water and the blood – it wasn't long till I recognised that the same kind of inspiration was reflected in many of the high crosses.

There are differences in the iconography because the Maghera lintel is so spacious and gives the artist untold scope for elaborate detail and symbolism, including gathering the disciples under the lengthened arms of Christ. There isn't the same space on the surface of a high cross, but it doesn't take a lot of space to show Christ between the two soldiers with the sponge and the spear. Some of the crosses show Christ in the undivided garment; some do not. There are other differences: on some of the crosses the arms of Christ are stretched out horizontally, while on the Cross of the Scriptures in Clonmacnois the arms of Christ are reaching down towards us, and on the unfinished cross in Kells one hand is lowered slightly towards us and the other is slightly raised towards heaven.

The remarkable thing is that while at first glance the crosses seem to follow a standard pattern, and we could assume that they are all basically the same, yet when we look at them more closely, each one is unique in its detail and its composition. The great Irish crosses, like the Book of Kells and the other illuminated manuscripts, beautifully perfect the tradition of broken symmetry, where there is an underlying unity of purpose and yet a variety of detail as vibrant as creation itself.

A high cross from Ahenny, Co. Tipperary

Chapter Three

Creative Energy

Crosses of the 9th and 10th centuries

Anyone who is interested in Irish art from the seventh century until the end of the twelfth century owes a deep debt of gratitude to Françoise Henry. Françoise was a French girl, and she was a student of art at the university of Paris when she met an Irish girl who had also come to Paris to study art. The Irish girl was Caroline (Carrie) Fitzgerald. She and Françoise became friends, and when the summer holidays came around, she invited Françoise to come to Ireland for a few weeks. Carrie was from Co. Tipperary, and she brought Françoise to see the high crosses at Ahenny. This French girl instantly fell in love with the Irish sculptures and the Irish landscape. She knew she wanted to make the study of early Irish art her life's work. She completed her studies, and then came back to Ireland, to University College, Dublin, and to a long and fruitful career in teaching art and in the interpretation and elucidation of the great works of early Irish art.

There is an extraordinary providence in Françoise Henry's coming to Ireland. It was the coincidence of her friendship with Carrie Fitzgerald which brought her there in the first place. Hilary Richardson writes:

This experience (seeing the crosses at Ahenny) may have been the initial stimulus but already the ground was well prepared. A set of extraordinarily happy circumstances converged to make this time propitious for such a study. Not only was Françoise Henry's personality and training eminently suitable for the task ahead: she came at a crucial moment in Irish history, when much of the older social heritage still remained, while at long last the value of Irish culture was beginning to be positively realised and appreciated. If she had come a little later much of the traditional life in rural Ireland, especially in the west, would have been less authentic. It is hard to imagine a more favourable combination of scholar, subject matter and exact timing. (Preface to vol. III, *Studies in Early Christian and Medieval Irish Art*, by Françoise Henry, London 1985.)

The training Françoise received in Paris from her teacher, Henri Focillon, could almost have been specifically designed for her work in Ireland. His study of Romanesque sculpture was based on close and in-depth analysis of form and spatial relationships, and his lecturing technique was based on involving his students in the process of analysis and elucidation. Françoise brought this skill and experience to her work on the Irish stone sculpture, and also to the metalwork and manuscript illumination. The day that Carrie brought her friend Françoise to see the high crosses at Ahenny, Co. Tipperary, was a blessed day for Françoise, because it pointed her to her life's work. It was also a blessed day for Ireland and for everyone who appreciates our rich heritage of stone and metal and manuscript art.

Françoise Henry

Françoise Henry's research and teaching proved to be a landmark in the study and awareness of early Irish art. She wrote many books and magazine articles on the subject, in French and in English. The results of her groundbreaking studies were gathered together in her *magnum opus*: a unique treatment of the sculpture, the metalwork and the manuscript illumination in three substantial and beautifully illustrated volumes published in London by Methuen and in New York by the Cornell University Press. *Irish Art in the Early Christian Period* appeared in 1965, *Irish Art during the Viking Invasions* appeared in 1967, and *Irish Art in the Romanesque Period* appeared in 1970. These volumes remain the standard and foundational work on early Irish Art, and have never been surpassed.

By the time I met Domhnall Ó Murchadha and his wife Máirín, these three beautiful books were already out of print. Domhnall and Máirín were close friends and colleagues of Françoise, and she had named them as executors of her will. When she died, they went to France to settle her affairs. When they returned they brought me a set of the three volumes which had been in her own possession, and on which she had made some corrections and annotations. I treasure them, and I have had them beside me as I worked on this little introduction to the great crosses.

Françoise named her second volume *Irish Art during the Viking Invasions*. The Viking warriors made ferocious attacks on the monasteries and on the country. The extraordinary thing is that it was during that period of continuing threat, instability and destruction that some of the very greatest works of our artistic and cultural heritage were created.

Kells

The island of Iona, off the coast of Scotland, was particularly vulnerable to attacks from the sea, and it was repeatedly and ferociously attacked by the Vikings between AD 801 and AD 804. It was for that reason that the monks abandoned their island monastery, which had been the headquarters of all the Columban monasteries. They came to Ireland and made their new headquarters at Kells, Co. Meath. Two reasons are suggested for the choice of Kells as a site for the monastery: it was on a height which could be easily defended, and it is believed that the monastery of Armagh gave some of its lands in the area for the new foundation. The great illuminated manuscript known as the Book of Kells was probably begun in Iona, and brought by the monks to their new home in Kells where it was completed. There are four highly-significant sandstone crosses in Kells: two of which are still complete, or nearly complete, one of which is unfinished and another broken. They are wonderful examples of the stone crosses of the ninth century, and it may be that it was here in Kells that a new flowering of the great scripture crosses began.

There is a cross near the round tower at the entrance to the monastic site which has a Latin inscription: 'Patricii et Columb(a)e crux'. Since Patrick and Columba are mentioned together, it may be that there is a reference here to the gift of land by Armagh for the new monastery of Columba, or at least a sign of unity between these important monasteries.

The cross of Patrick and Columba, Kells, Co. Meath

I really like the shape of this cross. The Kells crosses are distinctive and beautifully proportioned. On the west face of this principal cross Christ is shown in glory at the centre of the ring at the head of the cross, while there is an image of the crucifixion below. This suggests that the cross was carved early in the ninth century, because from now on the crucifixion will be placed on the head of the cross in the centre of the circle. The crucifixion had appeared on the shaft of the south cross at Clonmacnois and on the shaft of the cross at Moone, Co. Kildare and at Carndonagh, Co. Donegal.

On the east face of the cross of St Patrick and Columba, from the bottom upwards, we find Adam and Eve, Cain killing Abel, the young men in the fiery furnace, Daniel in the lions' den, the sacrifice of Isaac, Saints Paul and Anthony in the desert, a fish, and king David playing a musical instrument. There are no frames separating the panels on this cross, which gives an impression of free-flowing movement to the whole composition. The shaft of the cross widens slightly as it rises towards the circle at the top, which enhances the sense of movement.

Crosses were erected in and around the monasteries in the eighth century, particularly in the midlands and in the east and in the north. Many more were erected during the ninth and into the tenth century, in spite of the Viking raids. There was clear development in the making of the crosses also: the crosses are now taller; instead of geometrical decoration such as interlacing ribbons, the surface of the crosses is covered with human figures and biblical scenes. The sculptures are large in scale and impressive in style and technique. These crosses will stand out as wonders in the story of art, not just in Ireland but in the world.

There are times in politics or in art when an effective achievement stands out against the tide of history, to such an extent that it is difficult to offer any explanation other than the unconquerable human spirit. The sculpture of the high crosses in Ireland in the ninth century is such an achievement. The tide of history was against it; the armed force and ferocious violence of the Vikings was against it; the monks and all the local communities were seized with fear, so much so that they welcomed the worst weather because it would keep the Viking sailors off the rough seas:

> Is acher in gaíth in-nocht;
> fu-fuasna fairggae findfolt;
> ní ágor réimm mora minn
> dond láechraid lainn úa Lothlind.
> *(a note on the margin of a manuscript*
> *from the ninth century:*
> *Stiftsbibliothek MS 904, St Gallen.)*

> The wind is wild tonight;
> it tosses the white hair of the sea;
> I do not fear the coursing of the calm sea
> by the fierce Viking warriors.

In spite of all of that, extraordinary growth took place in Irish stonework. Remarkable developments took place in the making of the great crosses, and in the very life of the monasteries themselves. The unconquerable human spirit was at work, and along with it, or as part of it, there was a new surge of spiritual energy among the monks and the faithful people of the Irish Church. In the year AD 774 St

Maelruáin founded the monastery of Tallaght in Co. Dublin. He gathered a small group of monks around him, and they were full of the spirit of unity and of renewal, reminiscent of the words of the African St Cyprian, quoted more than once in the documents of Vatican II: '*ut fraternitatem in unum animatam*' – as a brotherhood enthusiastically striving for unity. They were referred to as *aontadh Mhaelruáin*, 'the unity of Maelruáin'.

Perhaps because of the political instability and the Viking threat, or perhaps because people were beginning to realise that the golden age of the Irish Church was heading for a crisis, huge numbers of people responded to the call for renewal. A movement of spiritual renewal spread around the country, the movement that came to be known as the 'Céilí Dé', the spouses or close friends of God. It was that movement, and the unconquerable human spirit, which underpinned the surge throughout the country which gave power and energy to spiritual and artistic creativity.

Two of the Kells crosses have defects: one is badly broken, with its top missing, and the other is unfinished. Of course it is a great pity that they are not complete, so that we could experience the full skill and creativity of the craftsmen who made them, and yet strangely it is these incomplete crosses which haunt my memory. Perhaps they remind us that it is more important to savour the qualities that are present, rather than lamenting what is missing.

The broken cross is unusual not only because it is broken, but because a single theme is emphasised in the remaining panels. That theme is the water of baptism: the baptism of

The Baptism of Jesus, from the broken cross, Kells

Adam and Eve, from the broken cross, Kells

Christ, the wedding at Cana (water changed to wine), the Samaritan woman (the well, and living water), the healing at the pool of Bethesda, the washing of the infant Jesus, Noah's Ark (saved from water), and the people of Israel crossing the Red Sea (saved through water). In 1963 the great Irish sculptor Oisín Kelly carved a beautiful baptismal font for the new church of St Theresa in Sion Mills, Co. Tyrone, with many of those same images in a continuous frieze around it.

The unfinished cross (which also appears on the cover of this book) is a dramatic and evocative image. The shape of the massive stone is almost complete, except for the top part of the cross and the two upper quadrants of the circle on either side of it. The break must have happened in the course of the stone carving, perhaps because of a hidden fault line in the stone. The sculptor then stopped what he was doing, his mallet poised in mid-stroke and his chisel set down. Thankfully, in spite of his frustration, he didn't destroy what he had already done. The shaft of the cross is carved into square and rectangular panels in relief, ready for the detail of the figures. It gives us a great insight into the technique and methodology of the stone workers. The image of the crucifixion at the head of the cross, luckily for us, had already been practically completed. It is a strong and beautiful image: Jesus is dressed in the long, undivided garment; his right hand is reaching down towards us, and his left hand is raised slightly towards heaven. Two angels hold Christ's head, which, unusually on the high crosses, appears to have a halo, and below his arms are the two soldiers with the sponge and the spear. It may be incomplete, but in its own way it is perfect.

The crucifixion, from the unfinished cross, Kells

There is another important cross in Kells. It is referred to as the Market Cross. Wherever it was originally, it was re-erected in 1688, at another time of social and political upheaval, and stands in the centre of the town. Even though the top is partly broken, it has the same beautiful outline and the same perfect proportions as the other great Kells crosses. These shapes did not happen by accident; they point to conscious, sophisticated design and careful, masterly execution.

One day Domhnall Ó Murchadha took me out to his studio and showed me a project he was working on: a comprehensive analysis of the geometry of all the great high crosses. He had laid out the plans of each high cross on a large rectangular board or heavy card. He was very excited by what he was discovering. The design of all the crosses was based on a system of measurements and proportions which were consciously and precisely planned, and followed classical patterns, including what is referred to as the golden mean. He showed me a board, on which he had drawn the outline of one of the crosses. He had erected a square on the horizontal line running from one arm of the cross to the other. He had then marked and measured the diagonal of that square. The length of the diagonal was exactly the length of the shaft of the cross. It is the interlocking measurements which create the tight and harmonious proportions of the crosses. They are not all identical, of course. For example, the shaft of the cross might be twice the length of the horizontal line across the arms. But they are inter-connected according to pre-planned measurements and proportions. Even the width of the cross-shaft and its depth relate in classical proportions.

Among the panels on the Market Cross in Kells are Adam and Eve, the sacrifice of Isaac, Daniel in the lions' den, Cain killing Abel, King David, the loaves and fishes, Saints Paul and Anthony, and on the head of the cross on the north face, the crucifixion. The crown of thorns is visible on the head of Christ, which is unusual on these crosses.

The crosses of Kells show all the signs of deep reflection on the scriptures, and the panels are arranged to indicate a process which finds its fulfilment in Christ crucified and in the Eucharist. The same emphasis underlies the carvings on a number of crosses in the north, including Clones, Ardboe and Donaghmore, and on the remnant of a cross in Armagh. Unfortunately, only broken fragments remain of some of the crosses, and though the Ardboe and Donaghmore crosses are almost complete, they were carved from a soft sandstone which has crumbled with weather and the passage of time, so that some of the detail is unclear.

Ardboe, Donaghmore and Clones
The cross of Ardboe is among the highest in Ireland. This cross and the cross of Muireadach (*The Cross of the Scriptures*) in Monasterboice are over twenty-two feet high. The cross of Ardboe is deeply rooted in the memory of anyone born and reared on the western shore of Lough Neagh. It is generally referred to in English as '*The Old Cross of Arboe*'. It may seem strange that local people have not shown great interest in the detail of the carving, though they would recognise the crucifixion scene in the centre of the ringed head. But this tall stone column with the form of the celtic cross is recognised as an important landmark,

The High Cross of Ardboe, Co. Tyrone

whether seen from the shore or from a boat on the lough. It gives identity to the physical landscape, but it is also an icon which persists in a landscape of faith, like a gateway leading to the rich traditions of the early Irish Church. The cross stands in a graveyard near the ruins of an old church, on land which once was an ancient monastic site.

Because the cross of Ardboe is so tall, there is space on the surface of the stone for a variety of sculptured panels. On one side there are images from the Old Testament: Adam and Eve, the sacrifice of Isaac, Daniel in the lions' den, the young men in the fiery furnace, leading up to images of Christ at the top – his second coming, and the Last Judgment. On the other side there are images from the New Testament: the Three Kings, the wedding at Cana, the loaves and fishes, Jesus entering Jerusalem, the scourging, and at the top the crucifixion according to John with the sponge and the spear. Jesus is dressed in the long, undivided garment, which is shown drawn in at or below the knees and flowing down like a dress. This is unique to the Ardboe cross, although a flaring dress form appears on some metal plaques of the period. There are sculpted panels on the narrow sides of the cross-shaft also.

The Donaghmore cross is on the street of the village, just where the road divides in two, so that the traffic flows by on either side continuously. This cross is a composite: the head came from one cross and the shaft from a different cross. They were erected as a single cross in 1776. In its present form, these images are visible: the shepherds, the kings, the baptism of Jesus, the wedding at Cana, Jesus entering Jerusalem, the loaves and fishes, the scourging, and at the top the crucifixion. On the other side there are: Adam and Eve, Cain killing Abel and the sacrifice of Isaac. It looks as if the original crosses would have been very like the cross of Ardboe.

There is a cross in Clones which is related to the other northern crosses. Nowadays the fame of Clones rests on its significance as an important centre for Gaelic games in Ulster. But its fame goes back a long way. St Tiarnach founded a monastery here, and there is a round tower on the site as well as the cross. Again, this is not a single complete cross: not only does the head of the cross not belong with the rest of the cross, but it doesn't even belong to the same period in history. The head of the cross was carved in the eighteenth century, which means we can disregard the head of the cross as far as the ninth century is concerned. The decoration and the sculpted images on the shaft of the cross link it to the Donaghmore cross.

Moone and Castledermot

If we continue our journey and travel south east, we find an important group of crosses in Co. Kildare which have an identity of their own. They are situated at Moone and at Castledermot, and they are carved, not from sandstone, but from granite, a much harder and long-lasting stone. The medium has its own effect on the sculpture, of course, because granite is a more difficult stone to carve. The name of Moone in Irish is Maoin Cholm Cille, and it was part of the *familia* of the Columban monasteries. Castledermot is the monastic site of Díseart Diarmada, and was part of the Céilí Dé renewal movement. The crosses of Moone and

The Moone Cross, Co. Kildare

Castledermot are related, not only because of the granite that was used for the carvings, but also because of the images and themes of the sculpture.

There has been a long-lasting argument about whether the high cross of Moone or the Castledermot crosses came first. I have no expertise to bring to bear on this question, but I was interested to read the views of Eoin de Bhaldraithe in a booklet from Bolton Abbey, Moone: *The High Crosses of Moone and Castledermot, a Guided Tour*. Eoin thinks that the work of more than one sculptor is reflected in the high cross of Moone. There was a cross in Moone dating from the end of the eighth century, he suggests. That would be in keeping with the date proposed by Françoise Henry. Then, in the ninth century, the crosses of Castledermot were carved. After that, a new base was added to the Moone cross, in a style that was based on the Castledermot crosses. There is something attractive about that proposition. It would explain the height of the Moone cross: it is very tall and slender, and in that respect unlike the usual proportions of the high crosses around the country. It would explain another thing as well: Christ appears raised up in glory at the head of the cross, with his arms stretched out, where we might expect to find the crucifixion. But the crucifixion according to John is now at the bottom of the cross-shaft, immediately above the famous panel of the twelve apostles. The argument about the dating of these crosses may continue for a long time yet, but there are certainly thematic links between them. On the Moone cross, and on the north cross, Castledermot, we find the crucifixion based on the passion narrative in the gospel of John, and near it the representation of the twelve apostles, indicating the

The North Cross, Castledermot, Co. Kildare
(The Crucifixion and the Twelve Apostles)

birth of the Church from the side of Christ on the cross, as we have seen on the Maghera lintel. In the Maghera Crucifixion the disciples are gathered together under the protective arms of Christ; on the Moone cross the panel with the twelve apostles is placed directly below the crucifixion image; and on the north cross in Castledermot the crucifixion according to John is at the centre of the circle at the head of the cross, surrounded by the twelve apostles, three on each arm of the cross. Whichever cross was carved first, it is clear that they are based on the same theology and the same ecclesiology.

The monastery of Díseart Diarmada (Castledermot) was founded in the year AD 812 by an Ulsterman, Diarmait Ó hAedo Róin, who had studied at the monastery of Bangor and was a member of the Céilí Dé renewal movement. There are two exceptional crosses on the site, one to the north and one to the south. On the north cross the crucifixion is at the centre of the head of the cross, surrounded by the twelve apostles. On the opposite side, behind the crucifixion, Adam and Eve represent the Fall which necessitated the redemptive sacrifice of Christ. On the shaft of the cross are: Saints Paul and Anthony, the temptation of Anthony, and Daniel in the lions' den. On the reverse side, along with Adam and Eve, we find King David playing the harp and the sacrifice of Isaac.

I have mentioned the theology underpinning the representation of the crucifixion on the high crosses, based on the passion story in St John's gospel. The other sculptured panels on the crosses are not random images: they too are underpinned by a series of ideas and inter-related stories and symbols. Some of these are:

1. Old Testament stories which pre-figure the saving work of Christ (for example, the sacrifice of Isaac, the son of Abraham).

2. Themes from the Liturgy, especially referring to Christmas (the infant Jesus) and to Easter (the Passion of Christ).

3. The Help-of-God stories (examples from the Old Testament and from the New Testament of the saving love of God, when God intervenes on behalf of his faithful people: Daniel in the lions' den, the young men in the fiery furnace, the Flight into Egypt).

The Flight into Egypt

4. Stories from the lives of the saints: for example, Saints Paul and Anthony in the desert (an example of the interest in the Irish monasteries in the monastic traditions of Egypt). Sculptures of the raven bringing food to the hermit St Anthony also have a Eucharistic symbolism.

The stories which are called the Help-of-God stories are very interesting. They are listed in the Stowe Missal (from the monastery of Maelruáin of Tallaght) and in Féilire Óengusa (The Martyrology of Oengus). Both books are dated c.AD 800 and have associations with the Céilí Dé. We have a version of the Help-of-God stories in present-day liturgical use in the Rite of Anointing of the Sick, in the prayers of intercession for a person who is dying:

Deliver your servant, Lord,
  as you delivered Noah from the flood.
Deliver your servant, Lord,
  as you delivered Abraham from Ur of the Chaldees.
Deliver your servant, Lord,
  as you delivered Job from his sufferings.
Deliver your servant, Lord,
  as you delivered Moses from the hand of Pharaoh.
Deliver your servant, Lord,
  as you delivered Daniel from the den of lions.
Deliver your servant, Lord,
  as you delivered the three young men from the fiery furnace.
Deliver your servant, Lord,
  as you delivered Susanna from her false accusers.
Deliver your servant, Lord,
  as you delivered David from the attacks of Saul and Goliath.
Deliver your servant, Lord,
  as you delivered Peter and Paul from prison.
  (Pastoral Care of the Sick: Commendation of the Dying)

The sculptors of the great crosses had the scriptures, the liturgy of Mass and the sacraments and the life of the Church as sources of inspiration. Images like Saints Paul and Anthony in the desert reflect monastic life and the spirituality of the Céilí Dé movement.

There is an element of paradox about the other cross at Castledermot, which is on the south side of the monastery. On one hand, the shape of the cross and the style of the granite carving are very like the north cross. It is easy to see that they belong to the same group or family of sculptures. On the other hand there are some noticeable differences. The east side of this cross has only geometrical shapes and interlace. On the west face there are: Daniel in the lions' den, the temptation of St Anthony, Adam and Eve, and Saints Paul and Anthony. The crucifixion is at the top, in the centre of the circle, with, on either side, King David playing the harp and the sacrifice of Isaac. The twelve apostles are still there, but on this cross they are almost hidden, creeping in pairs up the narrow south side of the shaft of the cross.

Monasterboice, Clonmacnois and Durrow

It was a moment of destiny for Françoise Henry when she came on holiday to Ireland and made contact with Ireland's heritage of art and architecture. She immediately realised that she had found her life's work. It was a moment of destiny for Irish art as well, and for everyone who wishes to appreciate Ireland's cultural heritage. She came from France, and she was able to cast an unbiased eye on the objects of her research. But she had a deep humanity, and an open, appreciative soul. Not only was she able to uncover the historical context and to identify with precision the quality of the works of art, but she could reach beyond the created work to connect with the artists who had created it.

Muireadach's Cross, Monasterboice: The Hand of God

I remember the first time I read her commentary on the Book of Kells. Until then I had looked in wonder at the amazing, colourful pages of illumination without even thinking about the people who were behind the work. My perception was completely transformed when Françoise told of the three great artists who had created some of the most beautiful pages of the Book of Kells: *The Goldsmith*, who produced pages like the famous Chi-Rho page: an intricate precise geometrical drawing with a dominant yellow reminiscent of gold; *The Portrait Painter*, who made wonderful icons of Christ and the Apostles – full pages on which a personalised portrait sits within a frame of geometrical patterns; and *The Narrator*, who pictured scenes from the life of Christ, his birth in the stable, the arrest of Christ by the soldiers, for example – using flowing freehand drawing with purples and greens that match and clash like a minor chord in music.

New depths of symbolism are always being discovered in these images: the picture I have called *The Arrest of Christ* may be even more fascinating than just a narrative moment. In the book, '*Treasures of Irish Christianity*', produced by Veritas at the time of the International Eucharistic Congress in Dublin in June 2012, Jennifer O'Reilly gives an intriguing and compelling analysis of the image. She draws attention to the symbolism of the red-vested Christ, with two attendants rather than captors, and the eucharistic overtones of the vines rising from chalices. If we accept her analysis, the imaginative and exciting liturgical symbolism is matched by the confidence of the unusual freehand swirl of the drawing and the dramatic intensity of the colouring. Even if Françoise Henry's term, *The Narrator*, proves to be somewhat of an understatement, this artist will remain my favourite among the masters of the Book of Kells.

The same humanity and depth of appreciation which Françoise displayed in her analysis of the illuminations in the Book of Kells is evident also in her treatment of the great crosses, especially when she writes about the four crosses which stand out in size and in significance among the great high crosses of Ireland: Muireadach's Cross and the Tall Cross at Monasterboice, the Cross of the Scriptures at Clonmacnois, and the Cross of the Scriptures at Durrow, Co. Offaly. Françoise doesn't propose any name for the artists in this case, but she is certain that the four crosses were sculpted by the same team of master stone carvers, which she calls *The School of Monasterboice*. One great master sculptor would have been in charge of the work and would have overseen the plan and the process leading to the perfection of the final detail. A team of highly-skilled stone carvers would have worked with him, and in the background would have been monks qualified in scripture, liturgy and theology.

Two developments are immediately apparent in these crosses:

a) Not only are they tall, and the Cross of Muireadach in Monasterboice is over 22 feet high, but they are massive – huge in every way, and the sculpture itself has reached new levels.

b) More themes are represented on the carved panels – there is more space for the panels on these huge crosses – and there is also a greater variety of themes.

Muireadach's Cross, Monasterboice, Co. Louth

These crosses were carved from a fine, hard sandstone with a greater quartz content, which made them lighter in colour than the northern crosses and better able to withstand the elements, so that they are still in good condition. The details of the carving can be clearly seen. These crosses were probably made under the patronage of Church leaders who were intent on renewal and reconstruction after the Viking raids. They wanted the monastic buildings to look their best, and they had round towers built to complete the sites and to protect them. For this and for the erection of impressive stone crosses they would have sought out the best master stone workers that could be found.

The team who produced the high cross of Muireadach at Monasterboice were not just the best that could be found: they had the confidence to tackle something bigger and more ambitious than had been seen before. The cross of Muireadach is massive, and yet this huge block of stone is handled with a lightness of touch which demanded discipline, totally professional skill and experience, as well as depth of inspiration. It is no wonder that Domhnall Ó Murchadha, in the Capuchin Annual in 1969, could refer to 'the high moments of the tenth century, when, as Dr Françoise Henry so beautifully puts it, monuments "like the crosses of Kells and Monasterboice appear as a magnificent preface to medieval sculpture"'.

At the head of Muireadach's cross, in the centre of the circle, on the west face there is the crucifixion and on the east face there is a representation of Christ at the Last Judgment. The crucifixion is, of course, based on the passion story according to John: the spear is piercing Christ's left side.

The Last Judgment scene is very interesting: the motif of Christ with the crossed rods – one finished in the shape of a cross and the other showing the flowering rod of Aaron – is based on an Egyptian image from the *Book of the Dead* of Osiris-Judge. It is fascinating to find an Egyptian motif on a stone cross in Co. Louth. It points to the extraordinary affinity between the Irish monasteries and the monasteries of Egypt. The Egyptian monks presumably Christianised the ancient Egyptian symbol, and then it was transferred to Ireland by contact between the monasteries.

Among the panels on the east face of Muireadach's cross are: Adam and Eve and beside them Cain killing Abel, David and Goliath, Moses striking the rock, the adoration of the three kings, St Michael, and, above the Last Judgment, Christ in glory and Saints Paul and Anthony. On the west face, in big square frames, are: the soldiers mocking Christ, the Risen Christ, and the *traditio clavium*, in which Christ gives the keys to Peter and the book of the New Law to Paul. On either side of the crucifixion are Peter's denial and the Resurrection. At the very top is the Ascension.

Among the images which are almost hidden on the cross, there is an interesting one under the arm of the cross on the south side: two animals which appear to be wrestling. Monasterboice is near the Cooley peninsula, famous as the setting for the epic *Táin Bó Cuailgne* ('The Cattle Raid of Cooley'). It has been suggested that it is the two bulls, the Finnbheannach and the Donn Cuailgne, that are fighting here on the narrow edge of the cross. If that is the case, we would have here another example of the sympathetic treatment of the ancient pagan stories, which were preserved on the manuscripts, painstakingly copied in the monasteries.

Muireadach's Cross, Monasterboice: Two animals fighting

The creativity and the flexibility of the artists can be seen in the images they chose to portray, but their achievement and their mastery of stone sculpture is evidenced also in the scale and proportions of the cross. When the master craftsman opted for a design that was larger and more massive than any previous cross, he had to adjust the measurements and the proportions to the scale of the new composition, and he succeeded perfectly. It is no wonder, if you are looking for a reproduction of an Irish cross, that Muireadach's Cross from Monasterboice is by far the most likely to be on offer.

The Tall Cross, Monasterboice

There is a second impressive cross in Monasterboice, which is called The Tall Cross. It is the highest of the crosses, but it looks even higher because it is slender in comparison to Muireadach's Cross. Once again, the crucifixion according to John is at the centre of the head of the cross. On the reverse, however, we do not find the Last Judgment on the Egyptian model. Instead, there is an unusual picture. It may be King David with his army, or it may well be Christ, presented as a victorious general bearing sword and shield, and surrounded by an army of followers. There are other additional images on the panels of this cross, some involving Moses and King David: David killing a lion, the sacrifice of Isaac, Moses striking the rock, Samuel anointing David, David with the head of Goliath, Samson, Elias, the three young men in the fiery furnace, Saints Paul and Anthony, the temptation of Anthony, and Christ saving Peter from the waves. On one of the narrow edges there is an image referring to John the Baptist, Zachariah and Elizabeth. On the same side as the crucifixion are: Christ in the tomb, the baptism of Christ, the women at the tomb, Christ with Peter and Paul, the Risen Christ, the undivided garment, soldiers, the arrest of Christ, the mocking of Christ, St Peter with a sword, and Pilate washing his hands.

Muireadach's Cross in Monasterboice is a massive landmark in the development of stone sculpture in pre-Norman Ireland. The same team of sculptors – the group which Françoise Henry called *The School of Monasterboice* – reached a new pinnacle of achievement in the Cross of the Scriptures at Clonmacnois. The cross was fashioned with originality and with wonderful craftsmanship from a single block of sandstone: an extraordinary feat. It is located on a bend of the river Shannon near Athlone, at the famous monastery of Clonmacnois, where the river is crossed by the ancient road of Eiscir Riada. The original Cross of the Scriptures has been taken indoors, into a custom built Visitors' Centre. A tall chamber surrounds the cross, with lighting from above and from the sides to accentuate the detail of the carving. A full-size replica has been positioned on the original site on the grass opposite the door of the cathedral church.

This is a unique cross, although it belongs in the tradition of the high crosses and reflects the characteristic style and execution of the School of Monasterboice. The arms of the cross are raised slightly towards the heavens – a feature not found on any other high cross. And this is the only high cross where the circle at the head of the cross is dominant. All the others have the cross dominant and the circle broken in four quadrants in the background. I have used the word circle, but this is a three-dimensional circle, a deep barrel of stone enclosing the centre of the cross. We are used to a front view of the cross, leaving the impression of two dimensions, but the last time I stood beneath the arm of the cross, looking upwards, I was amazed at the depth of the circle, jutting out beyond the arms of the cross. It reminded me of the effect of a car wheel when the steering wheel is fully turned to reveal the treads of a broad tyre.

This cross is big, and it is massively heavy. That's the most surprising thing about it: that the stone is so big, so heavy, so massive, and yet that the art is so fine and so light, and so full of movement. When you stand back to look at the cross, it rises up, lifts its arms towards the sky, while the arms

The Cross of the Scriptures, Clonmacnois, Co. Offaly

of Christ from the crucifixion icon stretch down towards you as if to raise you up towards him. Domhnall Ó Murchadha writes:

> Covered from base to top with a brocade of scriptural and other carvings, it never once gives the impression of complexity. Before it one can almost hear reiterated the oft-repeated saying of the masters of the Renaissance and of our own times: simplicity is the final seat of art. Here in this cross the master-sculptor has preserved the primal forms: prism, cube, cylinder, truncated pyramid: the essential elements of all classical art. He has set them together in marvellously measured proportions to form one harmonious whole. Attached to them, as it were, are the figured scenes. They grow out of the stone of the background and form an outer layer echoing the massive surfaces of shaft and wheel. The great Crucifixion echoes the simple geometry of the whole, bending the figure of the Redeemer to the architectural space. What matters here are the outstretched arms of redemption rather than the greater realism of a later time. (*Stone Sculpture in Pre-Norman Ireland*, The Capuchin Annual, 1969.)

Just as with Muireadach's Cross, the crucifixion and the Last Judgment are at the head of the Clonmacnois cross: on the west face – the first side to be seen by a person approaching the door of the cathedral church – the crucifixion according to John, and on the east face – nearer the door – the Last Judgment. The images of the Last Judgment, like Muireadach's Cross, are based on the motifs from the Egyptian Books of the Dead: an eastern iconography from the banks of the Nile now transplanted to the banks of the Shannon!

The west side of the Cross of the Scriptures is dedicated to themes associated with the Passion of Christ: Jesus entering Jerusalem, the scourging, the undivided garment, Christ in the tomb, the women at the tomb, the Resurrection of Christ (a rare image on the Irish crosses), and the Risen Christ. They relate very naturally to the glorious Johannine crucifixion on the west face, and to the Last Judgment and Christ in glory on the east face. There are themes from the Old Testament and Jesus with Peter and Paul on the east side of the cross-shaft.

The fourth cross from the School of Monasterboice stands on the monastic site of Durrow, Co. Offaly: Darmhagh Cholm Cille, a Columban monastery. The Book of Durrow, a beautiful illuminated manuscript, is associated with this site. As with Monasterboice and Clonmacnois, the crucifixion according to John and the Last Judgment with the Egyptian motifs are on reverse sides of the cross at the centre of the circle at the top. Again, on the west side of the shaft there are images relating to the Passion of Christ: the scourging, Peter denying Christ, the undivided garment, Pilate washing his hands, Christ in the tomb, and Christ with Peter and Paul. On the east side there are images from the Old Testament: David playing the harp, David killing a lion, the sacrifice of Isaac, and the Risen Christ. Muireadach's Cross at Monasterboice and the Cross of the Scriptures at Clonmacnois are at the pinnacle of pre-Norman sculpture in Ireland. They are breathtakingly beautiful. And yet the Cross of the Scriptures in Durrow more than holds its own: it is a jewel.

The Cross of the Scriptures, Durrow, Co. Offaly

The amazing achievement of the School of Monasterboice was to produce crosses which maintained the highest level of creativity and craftsmanship, but each of which had its own unique character and finish. It brings the 'broken symmetry' of celtic art to a new level. These achievements were not isolated works of genius which appeared out of the blue. The tradition of Irish stonework was built painstakingly over several centuries. Each step forward was appreciated and transmitted from mind to mind and from hand to hand, from master to apprentice. Every member of the stone squad of Ahenny, of Kells, of Armagh or Ardboe or Monasterboice was in training for superlative action. Domhnall Ó Murchadha reflected on the Cross of the Scriptures in Clonmacnois, and like the ancient Irish Annals he placed it in its historical context by reference to the local king Flann:

> When the High-King Flann Sinna died in 915 the art of the sculptured High Cross must have been nearing maturity. In the north the crosses of Armagh, Arboe, Kells, Monasterboice may well have been in process of construction or nearly complete. To the south and east the great crosses of Ahenny, of Kilcullen, of Moone were then well over a century in existence. Their combined achievement marked the evolution of design-powers in the arrangement of subject-matter and the treatment of materials that may be assumed to have originated with the incised grave-slabs common to monastic sites as far back as the late seventh century. At the end of Flann's reign, Ireland had already, in efforts extending over almost two and a half centuries of stone carving, established the first School of Sculpture in Western Europe. (*The Capuchin Annual*, 1969.)

On the crosses of the School of Monasterboice, in the representation of the crucifixion according to John, the spear is shown piercing the left side of Christ, i.e. it is on the right of the picture as we look at it. That is not always how the spear is depicted on the Irish crosses. The spear is on the right of Christ (on our left) on the Moone Cross, on the south cross at Castledermot, on the south cross at Clonmacnois, on the high cross of Ardboe, on the Maghera Crucifixion and on a number of metal plaques. Françoise Henry discusses some of the explanations that are put forward for this exceptional usage, exceptional if we take it as the norm that the spear should be seen piercing the *left* side of Christ – piercing his heart.

A metal plaque, showing the crucifixion according to John, with the spear piercing Christ's right side.

The two soldiers who wielded the sponge and the spear are not named in the gospels, but there is an old tradition that it was *Longinus* who stabbed Jesus with the spear and *Stephaton* who offered him the sponge. Françoise Henry says there was a tradition that Longinus was blind but that he was cured when the water and blood gushed over him from the side of Christ. For that reason, symbolically, Longinus might be taken to represent the Church, saved by the blood of Christ, and Stephaton, who offered him the sour wine, might be taken to represent the Jewish people. The suggestion is that Longinus was therefore honoured by being placed at Christ's right hand. Apart from the hint of anti-semitism, I have never liked that explanation.

A simpler and more biblical explanation is linked to the prophet Ezekiel. In Ezekiel 47:1 there is a description of the water flowing from the Temple:

> He brought me back to the entrance of the Temple, where a stream flowed eastwards from under the Temple threshold, for the Temple faced east. The water flowed from under the right side of the Temple, south of the altar. He took me out by the north gate and led me right round outside as far as the outer east gate where the water flowed out on the right hand side.

By portraying the water and the blood flowing from the right side of Christ, Christian artists were identifying the body of Christ with the Temple. Symbolically it was fitting that the blood and water should flow from the right side of Christ.

The inspiration that underlies the crucifixion images on the stone crosses also underlies the representation of the crucifixion on a number of metal plaques between the seventh and tenth centuries. The space on the plaques is limited, of course, and the crucifixion is the dominant central image. It is the crucifixion according to John, with angels supporting the head of Christ and the two soldiers holding the sponge and the spear. On several plaques, the spear is piercing the right side of Christ. He is shown wearing the undivided garment, which is sometimes elaborately decorated as a priestly vestment. The theology, especially the Christology and the ecclesiology, must have been deeply embedded in the mentality of the time, since it is expressed so widely and in such various art forms over several centuries.

Chapter Four

Change of Inspiration
The 12th century crosses

After the pinnacle of the stone carver's art represented by the School of Monasterboice, there is an unbelievable gap of more than a hundred years. How could the creative momentum that had been built up and so carefully fostered suddenly die without trace? In the first quarter of the tenth century, masterpieces of sculpture follow one another with no apparent inhibition. And then suddenly there are no more high crosses, as if the well had dried up. There is no easy explanation, but it was likely due to a mixture of causes from without and from within. The Viking warriors were attacking from the outside. There had been an interim of peace from the Viking attacks, but that came to an end in AD 913, and though Brian Boru eventually gathered the forces to defeat them at Clontarf in AD 1014, the social and political fabric of the country had been broken and distorted. From the inside, from the Church's point of view, it appears that the spiritual renewal of the Céilí Dé movement had faded. The Church of the eleventh century seemed to be drained of energy, waiting for a different form of renewal in the twelfth century.

The life of the Church persisted. The writing and illumination of manuscripts persisted. The art of metal-working persisted. There were large communities in the Irish monasteries across Europe, and monks came and went between them and the monasteries at home in Ireland. But the age of the great crosses was over. The Vikings renewed their fierce onslaughts again between AD 915 and AD 920. The great Scripture Cross of Durrow is dated around the year AD 930, and it stands as the last monument to the work of the master sculptors of that golden age of creativity. Over a hundred years would elapse before tall crosses would be carved again in Ireland, and when the new crosses arrived, they would have a different form and a different inspiration. They would also be sponsored by different patrons. They didn't appear at the instigation of monastic leaders or on the traditional monastic sites. Françoise Henry wrote:

> The conditions of artistic production are probably evolving during this period. Though the monasteries still play an essential part as patrons of art and nurseries of artists, the presence of lay craftsmen can be detected here and there and never before have kings relied so wholeheartedly on art as a source of prestige as they did in the twelfth century. The O'Briens at Killaloe and Limerick, Turlough O'Connor at Roscommon and Tuam, Cormac Mac Carthy in his kingdom of Desmond, and Dermot Mac Murrough in Ferns, play an essential part in the art of the late eleventh and twelfth centuries and loom very large in the story told in these pages. (*Irish Art in the Romanesque Period*, p. xiv.)

A huge change was taking place in the structures of the Church in Ireland at this time. In the twelfth century St Malachy (Maelmhaodhóg) was enthusiastically reorganising the Church according to the European system into dioceses and parishes. On journeys to Rome he used to stay at Clairvaux and he became friendly with St Bernard. He afterwards invited the Cistercians to come to Ireland. The new diocesan boundaries were agreed at the Synod of Rathbreasail (1111) and later at the Synod of Kells (1152). It was a process of renewal, and there was a fresh impetus in the life of the Church, inspired by St Malachy and St Laurence O'Toole, but the golden age of the Irish monasteries was over.

When the new high crosses were erected, they had no connection with the monasteries in which the scripture crosses were placed more than a hundred years before. There is no sign of these new crosses in Armagh, in Kells, in Clonmacnois or in Lismore or in any of the great monasteries previously referred to. There is a group of twelfth-century crosses in Connacht, under the patronage of king Turlough O'Connor: there are fragments in Tuam and in Cong. There is another group, under the patronage of the kings of Munster: in Cashel, in Roscrea, in Monaincha (Móin na hInse) in Co. Tipperary, and in Dysert O'Dea. There are crosses at Kilfenora in Co. Clare, and on Inis Mór, on the Aran Islands. There is an isolated cross, known as the Market Cross, in Glendalough in Co. Wicklow.

On the Tipperary crosses at Cashel, Roscrea and Monaincha, there is a large figure of Christ in a long garment, which Françoise Henry suggests may be based on the Lucca Cross, a famous European wooden cross which was a favourite with pilgrims. Versions of it occur all over western Europe. Domhnall Ó Murchadha says:

Cross at Kilfenora, Co. Clare

A remarkable plastic change takes place in the next stage of Irish High Cross sculpture, in the early twelfth century. The intervening period that began with the resumption of the Viking wars may be responsible for the apparent absence of the new and original design that had marked the earlier work. It is possible that many of the carvers, during the troubled century that followed 914, left to find work on the new monuments of a Europe preparing the Romanesque ... When we can again begin to date our crosses, their appearance has changed considerably. Against the traditional wheeled arrangement figures carved half-round stand out, giving the whole monument a more complex aspect. The twelfth-century grit crosses of Tuam and Roscrea and the limestone monuments of Kilfenora and Dysert O'Dea suggest a different plastic vision. The projections of figures in fairly strong relief make for a more complex plan. ('Stone Sculpture in Pre-Norman Ireland', *The Capuchin Annual*, 1969.)

The cross at Dysert O'Dea is in good condition, and it is tall, and massively impressive. It was carved from a lovely Co. Clare limestone. On the east face of the cross are two figures in deep relief: above, Christ on the cross, and immediately below, an episcopal figure wearing a mitre and holding a crozier. The right hand, which would usually have been raised in blessing, is missing, leaving a hole in the sculpture where it would have been attached. There are some other carved panels, but the style is very different from the panels on the tenth century scripture crosses. Adam and Eve are surrounded by exotic foliage, and in the panel showing Daniel in the lions' den, the lions metamorphose into strange animals caught in interlacing serpents. On the west face of the Dysert O'Dea cross there are panels of geometric designs and animal interlace. The break in continuity of the designs suggests that the two pieces of the cross were not originally meant to be integrated. The centre top of this side of the cross is filled with five diamond shapes arranged in the shape of a St Brigid's cross, probably the earliest recorded example of a shape more usually created in straw or rushes.

At Kilfenora there are crosses which were carved from light-grey Liscannor limestone from the quarries about eight miles away. The Kilfenora monastery must have been significant in the twelfth century, because it was established as an episcopal see at the Synod of Kells in 1152. One of the most striking crosses stands on the green near the ruins of the Kilfenora cathedral. At the top is the figure of the crucified Christ wearing a long garment. A double line runs from a small triangular ledge under the feet of Christ to a larger triangle at the foot of the cross. On both sides of the double line, and on the back of the cross, there is geometrical decoration. A second complete cross survives here also. It is called the Doorty cross, after a local family. The carving on this cross is very unusual. On one side at the top of the cross there is the figure of Christ. On the other side, at the top, there is an episcopal figure wearing a pointed mitre and holding a crozier. Under the feet of this figure there is a rather grotesque representation: two figures (Saints Paul and Anthony?) plunging their croziers into a weird animal.

There is an unusual cross at Cashel, on the mound traditionally associated with the inauguration of the Munster kings. Domhnall Ó Murchadha comments:

The Doorty Cross, Kilfenora, Co. Clare

It is much worn and a considerable portion has been broken off. The faces of the figures too on the east and west sides have been mutilated. Enough remains to tell us how wonderfully these sculptors had designed this new and daring monument ... The central shaft of the Cashel Cross carries what must have been the highest plastic achievement in sculpture of the twelfth century, the integration of two full-length figures with the whole mass-design. To the west the fully-clothed figure of Christ with outstretched arms and robe girdled at the waist; to the east a noble figure wearing a chasuble and carrying in his hand a bishop's crook, complete the cross form of the upper portion of the monument. The figures stand on corbelled animal heads, reminding one of the figures on a transition or very early Gothic porch sculpture of the Continent. In a cross or raking light at Cashel it is possible to trace the spiral curving lines that were the decorative treatment of portal figure-drapery in twelfth-century continental work. The great wooden cross at Lucca has been suggested as a prototype for this draped figure of Christ. Whatever the influences may have been on sculptors working in Cashel in the twelfth century, the masters who carved this monument from the local stone of the Drumbane sandstone district invented their own distinctive design. There were, of course, draped rood figures in pre-Norman England but no complete and complex unit as daring as this. ('Stone Sculpture in Pre-Norman Ireland', *The Capuchin Annual*, 1969.)

There is a paradox in these twelfth-century crosses. On the one hand they are high crosses, demonstrating creativity and masterly craftsmanship – amazingly after the Viking destruction and the absence of anything of this kind for over a hundred years. Domhnall Ó Murchadha found them

The Cross of Cashel, Co. Tipperary

extraordinarily impressive, and writes of them with a feeling and an understanding which could only come from a master stone carver, and from one who lectured for many years on the history of Irish and European art.

On the other hand, there is a vast change from the spirit and the inspiration of the scripture crosses of the ninth and tenth centuries. The style of the sculpture has changed: there is exotic foliage and strange animals; the sculptors were so interested in dramatic depth of forms that they became impatient with the restrictions of a single block of stone and attached further pieces to the main sculpture, some of which have become detached through time and have been lost. However, there is a more fundamental difference: there is a difference in the thought, a difference in the underlying theology, especially in the ecclesiology – in what they imply about the Church. The figure of Christ on these crosses is still Christ raised up in glory, and to that extent they retain a link with the passion story in John's gospel. But the sponge and the spear are gone, and the apostles and the disciples and the signs of the community of the Church are gone. This is no longer an ecclesial crucifixion. The only symbol of the Church that remains is one isolated episcopal figure.

What does this episcopal figure stand for? Peter Harbison conjectured that it might represent the local saint, or the original founder of the monastery. Françoise Henry says:

> The question arises of who is meant by the ecclesiastic holding a crozier of a type unusual in Ireland who almost always accompanies the representation of Christ on the cross in monuments of this group. He can hardly be meant

Cross at Dysert O'Dea, Co. Clare

for a local saint, as he appears in widely different places. Any attempt at associating him with the establishment of new bishoprics in 1111 and 1152 would be discouraged by the fact that he appears at Dysert O'Dea and Killeany, two monasteries which did not become episcopal sees. One may wonder if what is meant is not a representation of Christ as Abbot of the World, a title given to him in some Irish texts. Comparisons may also come to mind with the Continental late twelfth-century enamelled crucifixes which often bear a figure of St Peter below the Crucifixion, an iconography which may be older than the actual surviving enamelled crosses. In Ireland the figure never holds keys, but the Kilfenora tiara, so similar to a pope's tiara, could give some weight to this hypothesis. (*Irish Art in the Romanesque Period*, pp 139–40)

Whether we think of this figure as a pope or a bishop, it represents a fundamental change in the iconography of the crosses. Where we once had a full representation of the passion narrative according to John, the sponge marking the death of Jesus and the giving of the Spirit, and the spear, the water and the blood marking the birth of the Church from the side of Christ, and the disciples – gathered under the lengthened arms of Christ as at Maghera, or encircling the crucified Christ like an apostolic halo as at Castledermot, or as a panel of apostles immediately below the crucifixion as at Moone – we now have a single isolated cleric as the remaining symbol of the Church.

Just when we have identified clear lines of demarcation between the earlier and the later crosses, history throws in an element of complexity. There is a high cross at Drumcliff which seems to cross the line of demarcation. And there is a cross-shaft at Boho, Co. Fermanagh, and a fragment of a

Cross at Drumcliff (East face), Co. Sligo

Cross at Drumcliff (West face), Co. Sligo

cross at Durrow. Françoise Henry calls these 'transitional crosses'.

At Drumcliff, on the head of the cross on the west face there is the crucifixion according to John, and on the east face the Last Judgment, all in keeping with the crosses of the ninth and tenth centuries. But on the shaft of the cross, as well as scriptural themes such as David and Goliath, a couple of panels of the holy family, or perhaps John the Baptist with his parents, and Adam and Eve, there are two strange animals, one like a lion and one like a camel, bursting out of the restricting lines of the low relief carving as bold projections. In the Adam and Eve panel, the branches of the tree are woven in decorative swirls above and below, and the serpent slithers up through the foliage, in keeping with the style of the twelfth-century crosses. There may be a simple explanation: Peter Harbison says that there are marks on the shaft of the cross that suggest it was adapted slightly to fit a head which did not originally belong with it. Also, the head of the cross is slightly darker in colour than the shaft, pointing to a later combination of parts of what were originally separate crosses: a twelfth-century shaft and a ninth- or tenth-century head. Both elements show wonderful craftsmanship, and together perhaps remind us that reality has a habit of breaking out of the simplicity of our favourite theories.

Chapter Five

Afterword
St Brigid's Cross and Penal Crosses

Because the great high crosses of Ireland were made from stone, a material which was capable of surviving wind and weather and lasting through many centuries down to our own time, we can examine the crosses, learn to interpret the carvings, and trace the inspiration of the sculptors. In that way, we can read in the crosses the theological and scriptural influences which guided the master craftsmen. We can identify the Christology and the ecclesiology of the early Irish Church, the living tradition of the monastic communities which were the birthplace of the great crosses.

There is another type of cross which is deeply-rooted in the Irish tradition, and has been handed down to our present generation: the St Brigid's Cross. There is an amazing paradox about the St Brigid's Cross. It is made of throw-away material like rushes or straw, and yet this biodegradable cross has survived the centuries with a persistence which rivals the permanence of the stone crosses. The durable material has preserved the crosses of stone; the crosses of straw and rushes have been preserved, not by the material, which is transient, but by the persistence of a living faith.

St Brigid's Crosses

Another typically Irish cross, the Penal Cross, is time limited in more ways than one. It is associated with a particular period, with the suffering of Penal Times and the Great Famine. It has a more limited survival time than the stone crosses, and is not reproduced annually (or generally into our own times) like the St Brigid's Cross. However, though made of wood and associated with a very difficult time in Irish history, of perhaps 10,000 examples originally produced, a few hundred have survived, many of them in remarkably good condition.

The St Brigid's Cross

St Brigid was born in the fifth century and died in the sixth century in the year AD 524. She founded a monastery at Kildare, and even what remains of the site today bears eloquent witness to the significance of the foundation. Naturally, it is not only a pilgrimage site but also a tourist destination, and as the visitor approaches up the hill the present stone structure of the Church of Ireland marks where the ancient Oak Church (*Cill Dara*) would have stood, and behind it a tall, well-preserved round tower dominates the scene. The land slopes away on one side to where the monastery of the men was located, and on the other side to the monastery of the women. The scale of the complex makes it easy to identify with the tradition that St Brigid won a generous grant of land from the local king against his will: it is said he offered her as much land as her cloak would cover, upon which she spread out her cloak and it miraculously extended in all directions to claim the magnificent site on which she based her monastery. Another tradition tells that she gave away her father's sword to a poor beggarman who asked for alms. The sword was encrusted with jewels, and had great value. But as well as providing wealth for the poor man, it also came to symbolise Brigid's opposition to the violence which the sword represented.

The St Brigid's Cross embodies another of the foundational stories of this national saint. The story goes that Brigid visited a local pagan king on his deathbed. She told him about Jesus Christ, and as she talked she lifted rushes from the floor covering around his bed, and wove them into the shape of a cross. She explained to the king that Jesus had died on the cross for our salvation. The king was converted and was baptised before he died. That moment of conversion lives on in the annual custom of making the St Brigid's Cross from rushes or straw. The crosses are made on the eve of St Brigid's feast, which is on the First of February, the first day of Spring. Prayers are said, and often the crosses are blessed at the Mass of the Feast. In many parishes there is a conscious effort to hand on the tradition, and adults teach the young people how to make the rush crosses, at school or at a parish gathering.

Fr Seán Ó Duinn OSB in his book, *The Rites of Brigid*, mentions seven types of St Brigid's Cross. The most common throughout Ireland is made by tying two sticks of wood in the shape of a cross, and weaving a diamond or lozenge shape at the centre with rushes or straw. Sometimes smaller diamond shapes are woven on each arm of the cross to complete a symmetrical cross of five straw lozenges, in the shape which appears in stone on the twelfth century cross of Dysert O'Dea.

In County Derry it is more usual to find crosses woven from rushes, without any wooden rods. The St Brigid's Cross is a beautiful symbol of the family and the Church. Every rush depends on the other rushes, so that the woven square at the centre suggests inter-dependence and unity, while the four arms of the cross reach out to the four corners of the earth.

In the Irish language version of the Marriage Rite of the Catholic Church in Ireland there is a beautiful blessing which can be used as the final blessing of the wedding Mass. The words in Irish go back for centuries. When a couple were getting married, their parents would take a St Brigid's cross which had been hanging in their home, and present it to the young couple to hang in their home. It became a symbol of handing on the traditions of the family and the traditions of the Faith. The tradition of the St Brigid's Cross is alive and well in the parish of Greenlough, and couples getting married very often incorporate this blessing into their wedding ceremony. A parent or parents usually carry up the cross in procession and hand it to the bride and groom to hold between their joined hands during the final blessing. Afterwards they bring it to their own home. This is the blessing, first in the original Irish:

C.   Go raibh an Tiarna libh.

P.   Agus le do spiorad féin.

C.   Síocháin an Athar libh,
           Síocháin Chríost libh,
           Síocháin an Spioraid libh,
           Gach lá agus oíche. Amen.

P.   Gach lá agus oíche. Amen.

C.   Coimirce an Athar oraibh,
           Coimirce Chríost oraibh,
           Coimirce an Spioraid oraibh,
           Gach lá agus oíche de bhur saol. Amen.

P.   Gach lá agus oíche de bhur saol. Amen.

C.   Beannacht an Athar oraibh
           Beannacht Chríost oraibh,
           Beannacht an Spioraid oraibh,
           Go coróin na beatha síoraí. Amen.

P.   Go coróin na beatha síoraí. Amen.

C.   Bail ó Dhia oraibh ó Shamhain go Lá 'le Bríde,
               ó Lá 'le Bríde go Bealtaine,
               ó Bhealtaine go Lúnasa,
               is ó Lúnasa go Samhain;
         is go mbeannaí Dia uilechumhachtach sibh,
         Athair, Mac agus Spiorad Naomh.

P.   Amen.

C.   The Lord be with you.

P.   **And with your spirit.**

C.   May the peace of the Father, the peace of Christ,
      the peace of the Spirit be with you,
      every day and night, Amen.

P.   **Every day and night, Amen.**

C.   May you be in the care of the Father,
      in the care of Christ,
      in the care of the Spirit,
      every day and night of your lives, Amen.

P.   **Every day and night of your lives, Amen.**

C.   May the blessing of the Father, the blessing of Christ,
      the blessing of the Spirit be upon you,
      till you win the crown of eternal life, Amen.

P.   **Till you win the crown of eternal life, Amen.**

C.   May God bless you from All Souls' Day
      to St Brigid's Day,
              from St Brigid's Day to May Day,
              from May Day to Lammas,
              and from Lammas to All Souls'.
      And may almighty God bless you,
      the Father, the Son and the Holy Spirit.

P.   **Amen.**

A Penal Cross

The Penal Crosses

The penal crosses, or penal crucifixes, are identified with a particular period in Irish history. The Franciscans in Rosnowlagh, Co. Donegal, have a cross with the date 1702 inscribed on the back. Examples occur throughout the eighteenth century and into the nineteenth. The cross kept at the old Drumragh church in the Omagh parish is dated 1727. The Greenlough Cross is inscribed 1760. Though sometimes imitated, the original penal crosses peter out around 1830. They were carved from wood, and each one is made from a single piece of wood. Most of them are quite small – the largest recorded is sixteen inches tall, and most of them range from eight inches to eleven inches. The figure of Christ, stripped and crucified, is carved on them, wearing a loincloth rather than the long undivided garment which featured on the great stone crosses of the early Irish Church. The pieces of wood are narrow, which means that the arms of Christ are short and raised diagonally towards the upper corners of the crossbeams, to get the best use of the limited surface area. They are very light and portable.

A system of stylised symbols is used on the penal crosses, not invented by the woodcarvers who made the crosses, but drawn from sets of symbols which were in common use throughout Europe since the Middle Ages. They are symbols of pain, of the suffering of Jesus during his Passion and Crucifixion. At the period in history when the people of Ireland were suffering from famine and the pressure of the Penal Laws, they could identify with Jesus suffering on the Cross. Instead of the image of Jesus raised up in glory on the Cross, as we have in the Gospel of John and on the great scripture crosses, the carvers of the Penal crosses turned to the image of Jesus forsaken, isolated on the Cross and surrounded by the symbols of suffering, much closer to the Passion narrative in the Gospel of Mark: 'My God, my God, why have you forsaken me?'

Among the symbols which regularly recur on the penal crosses, there are the following, numbered on the drawing on page 117:

1.   Three squares (= dice, 'and for his clothing they cast lots');
2.   Pincers (for pulling out nails);
3.   A hammer;
4.   The sun, the moon, and sometimes stars;
5.   A halo;
6.   Cords;
7.   Veronica's towel;
8.   A chalice, or a jug;
9.   A ladder;
10.   A spear;
11.   A skull and crossbones;
12.   A rooster;
13.   A cooking pot;
14.   Three nails;
15.   Whips for the scourging.

Nearly all the symbols relate to the suffering and the Passion of Jesus. The rooster and the cooking pot are the exception, because they are symbolic of the Resurrection. This symbol goes back to the 'Gospel of Nicodemus' in the fourth century. According to the legend, after the death of Jesus Judas came home to his wife looking for a rope with

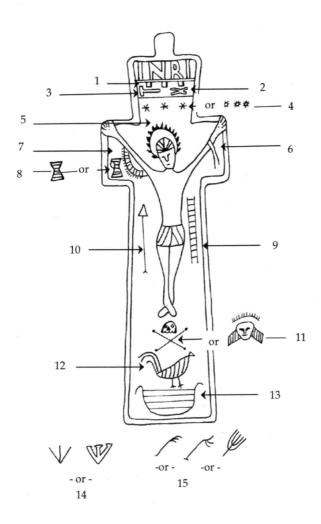

Penal Cross, with traditional symbols

which to hang himself. She had a rooster boiling in a pot over the fire. When Judas told her he was planning to kill himself, she said: 'Don't be a fool. Why would you do that?' Judas said: 'Jesus will rise from the dead, and I'll be in trouble.' 'Have sense, man,' said his wife. 'Jesus will no more rise from the dead than that rooster will rise out of the cooking pot and crow.' At that, the rooster rose out of the pot and crowed. The story is still told in Irish by the storytellers in the Donegal Gaeltacht, who claim that when the cock crowed, he did so in fluent Irish, saying: *Mac na hÓighe slán, Mac na hÓighe slán* ('The Son of the Virgin is safe')!

A.T. Lucas researched the background to the penal crosses in 1954. He believed that over ten thousand of the crosses may well have been carved, though only about four hundred are known today. They are found in south Ulster, north Connaught and north Leinster. He was certain that they were all associated with Lough Derg, and that pilgrims visiting Lough Derg would have brought a penal cross home with them after their penitential pilgrimage. One of the most poignant references to a penal cross comes from the story of the boat accident on Lough Derg in 1795. The boat overturned and the pilgrims were drowned. When the bodies were recovered, one girl was found with her little penal cross still clutched in her hand. That cross is still preserved in the basilica on Lough Derg. The girl was from the Derry Diocese. She was Mary O'Donnell from the parish of Aghyaran in Co. Tyrone. The date carved on the back of her penal cross was 1792.

The image of the penal cross is appropriate to the penitential spirit of Lough Derg, but it is also significant that Irish people turned to an image of the Crucifixion which evokes the isolation and suffering of the Passion narrative in the Gospel of Mark – Jesus forsaken, and the symbols of pain – at a time when they themselves were suffering from poverty and persecution. Against that background, I am intrigued by the apparition of Our Lady at Knock on a wet Thursday evening in August 1879. No word was spoken, there was no verbal message. The apparition at Knock communicates visually, and the visual message is Johannine: we speak of the apparition of Our Lady, which is accurate, but Our Lady did not appear alone. Along with Our Lady, the fifteen observers saw St Joseph, St John the Evangelist, and, centrally, the image of the altar and the Lamb. And to underline the presence of the heavenly as well as the earthly Church, there was the overarching vision of tremulous angels.

Into the midst of a suffering Church, appropriately symbolised by the little wood carvings of Mark's Passion narrative, materialises an image which would have seemed more at home in the golden age of the ninth- and tenth-century Irish Church. The early Irish Church was fascinated by the vision of St John: Jesus raised up in glory on the Cross, surrounded by his disciples, the altar and the Lamb of John's Apocalypse, the angels of God ascending and descending upon the Son of Man.

Was God reminding the people of Ireland that the glory is hiding at the very heart of the pain, that beyond the Cross there is the Resurrection? I am tempted to see in the visual message of the Knock apparition an echo of the visual message of that great icon, the Christ of Maghera, evoking the Passion narrative of John: Jesus at the very moment of death reigning as King on the Cross – *Mac Dé Bhí, Rí na Rún (Son of the Living God, King of the Mysteries)* – the cross itself, and the circle of the composition, sweeping the disciples and even the soldiers with sponge and spear into the angelic company: *coinne na hEaglaise neamhaí agus talúnda*, the meeting place of the heavenly and earthly Church.

We have a penal cross in Greenlough parish, generally referred to, appropriately enough, as the Greenlough Cross. The date 1760 is inscribed on the back. It was 250 years old in 2010, and we had a special celebration. Bill Bolger designed a beautiful set of parish stationery for us, using a photograph of the Greenlough Cross as a logo on the letterhead, compliment slip, and on the weekly parish newsletter – a kind of corporate image. When our St Oliver Plunkett church was being renovated in 2006, Fr Art O'Reilly, then Parish Priest, the parish Building Committee and the architect, Michael Hegarty, wanted a crucifix for the back wall of the sanctuary. They settled on a large replica of the Greenlough Cross, and it was carved by a young Slovakian called Aurél Bakulár.

He had come to Ireland, and had found work with a local firm, Rocks Joinery. It was providential for both parties, because Rocks Joinery had the trade connections and Aurél Bakulár had the woodcarving talent and skill in his family background. He did an exceptionally beautiful job on the penal crucifix. He has since returned to Slovakia, but he

The Greenlough Penal Cross

came back for a couple of weeks' holiday in 2010 to visit his friends and former colleagues. He came to the church one day to see how the cross looked, now that it was mounted on the wall. He was understandably delighted with it. He had chosen to carve the replica crucifix in Chinese tulipwood, because it has a resin which rises to the surface and creates a natural polished effect, a patina. What he didn't know was that the only reason Chinese tulipwood was available in Ireland was because it had been introduced by the world famous botanist Augustine Henry, a Greenlough man. That was providential also: a crucifix for the church in Greenlough parish, carved by a craftsman who just happened to be passing through, in a special wood which was available because of the skill and foresight of a native of Greenlough.

People nowadays can more easily appreciate the wooden penal crosses and the St Brigid's crosses made from straw or rushes. But some explanation and education is needed in order to appreciate the riches and the variety of the tradition of the great stone crosses. I spent two weeks in the Redemptorist monastery in Esker, Co. Galway, when I was working on the original Irish language version of this book. Fr Gerry Crotty, a retired theologian who has since died, was very interested in what I was doing. He spoke of the theology which was hidden in the high crosses, and he was delighted that the evidence of the thoughts of the early Irish monks and of the ideas of the master sculptors lived on to the present day because they had expressed their theology – particularly their Christology and their Ecclesiology – in a lasting medium. One evening at tea he looked across the table at me with some excitement in his eyes, like a man about to start a crusade: 'We have the evidence', he said; 'We need to raise the awareness.'

Touching a Living Tradition

I entered St Patrick's College, Maynooth as a student for the priesthood for the Diocese of Derry in September 1958. We were only a few weeks in Maynooth when Pope Pius XII died. Pope John XXIII was elected to succeed him. Pope John was seventy-six years old when he was elected, and his health wasn't that good, so people thought he would be a caretaker Pope, doing very little but just keeping things ticking over for the next man. They were seriously mistaken! He was only a couple of days in office when he began to talk about calling an ecumenical council of all the bishops of the Church throughout the world. He announced it in the Spring of 1959, and after a few years of preparation and consultation the Second Vatican Council was opened on 11 October 1962. It lasted until 1965, the year I was ordained, and all our years of study in Maynooth were affected by the excitement that accompanied the Council. It seemed as if the whole Church was filled with a new energy and inspiration.

Before beginning my theological studies in 1961–62 I had completed a degree in Celtic Studies. Fr Donnchadh Ó Floinn was our professor of Modern Irish, but as well as teaching the language he introduced us to the values and culture of the early Irish Church. He had written a number of articles on the subject. They were gathered into book form and published by Cumann na Sagart in 2006. Some of the articles were written in Irish, but one key document was written in English. It was called *The Integral Irish Tradition*, and summarised Fr Donnchadh's reflections on the heritage of faith which had been transmitted over the generations from the early Irish Church to our own day. He drew attention to three characteristics of the early Irish Church:

1. A great reverence for the Scriptures and for the Tradition of the Church;

2. A deep sense of the Communion of Saints, and of the unity of the members of the Church, especially at prayer. There was no private spirituality;

3. An understanding of the continuity of the life of the Church: that they were part of an unbroken chain. They appreciated the signs of God's grace in the centuries past, and had a firm hope that such signs would be experienced again. This conviction nourished their great missionary spirit.

When young theology professors like Enda McDonagh and Kevin McNamara shared with us the news from Rome and the vision of the Church that was coming through the documents of the Vatican Council, I recognised many of the qualities of the early Irish Church that Fr Donnchadh had talked about. It was as if we were reclaiming our heritage and making contact with a tradition that was not a fossil from the past, but living and vibrant – and our own.

When I look now at the great Irish crosses from the seventh to the tenth century, I see again the vision of the early Irish

Church which Fr Donnchadh Ó Floinn described, and I recognise the vision of the documents of the Second Vatican Council. None of these things are of merely academic historical interest. The sense of community – *muintearas* – in the early Irish Church is recognisable in the theme of communion so much emphasised by Pope John Paul II and Pope Benedict XVI. This sense of communion does not just imply a vague feeling of togetherness, but should be reflected in the way we treat one another, and in the very structures of the Church. At the opening of the Pastoral Convention of the Diocese of Rome in 2009, Pope Benedict said:

> It is necessary to improve pastoral structures in such a way that the co-responsibility of all the members of the people of God in their entirety is gradually promoted, with respect for vocations and for the respective roles of the consecrated and of lay people. This demands a change in mindset, particularly concerning lay people. They must no longer be viewed as 'collaborators' of the clergy but truly recognised as 'co-responsible' for the Church's being and action, thereby fostering the consolidation of a mature and committed laity. (*Church Membership and Pastoral Co-Responsibility*, 26 May 2009.)

Religious sociology in the twentieth century established that the elements of this vision were hugely significant for the survival and the flourishing of the Church. Fr Michael Paul Gallagher SJ was interested in what had happened to the Church in French-speaking Canada. French Canada was similar to Ireland in that there had been a very high percentage of religious practice in the Catholic parishes. Then, suddenly, within ten years the practice levels dropped from over ninety percent to less than forty. Fr Michael Paul had the insight to realise that what had happened in French-speaking Canada might well happen in Ireland. He did a detailed study of the French Canadian parishes, using the professional techniques of survey and analysis, to isolate the factors which had caused this change. He surveyed the parishes where practice had dropped, but he also surveyed a number of parishes where the high practice level had remained constant, and he compared the one to the other. He found certain common factors in the parishes which had kept a high level of practice, and he described this cluster of factors as a 'map of faith maturity'.

These factors included the experience of faith community, as opposed to a 'me and Jesus' private spirituality. The second factor was prayer. Where there was a real community of faith it expressed itself in prayer, personal and communal, in the family and in the public liturgy of the Church. Healthy prayer led to the third factor: genuine conversion to the person of Jesus Christ. Conversion then expressed itself in commitment: commitment to Christ flowing into commitment to the community, renewing the community of faith which nourished and transmitted personal faith, within the community and beyond to the next generation. Faith flowed continuously in this cycle of community, prayer, conversion and commitment. Where one element was missing or weakened, the whole cycle was at risk. Where two or more elements were missing, practice would begin to fail, and where practice failed, gradually faith itself would fail.

I have worked a lot over the years with Fr Johnny Doherty CSsR. With my brother Tony and Paddi Coyle we have been providing a support programme to parishes in the Derry Diocese for the development of parish pastoral councils. Part of our programme involves a residential weekend training workshop for newly-established pastoral councils. On these weekends one of the themes which inevitably recurs is the continuity of faith and practice. I had told Johnny about Fr Michael Paul Gallagher's work, and about the map of faith maturity. Johnny developed his own presentation of the map of faith maturity for the pastoral councils. Listening to him on one occasion, I quickly realised that he was saying something very important, so I wrote down as much as I could of what he was saying.

He drew a rough circle, showing the elements of faith maturity flowing around the circle. As he spoke, I drew the circle on my notebook, and added the words and phrases to the circle. The words on the right, on top and on the left suggested the shape of a cross. There were more words at the bottom, filling out the conversion to Christ in various aspects. As I added more and more phrases, the column of words stretched down the page, until I had a celtic cross of words. I found that very appropriate, as the themes of the map of faith maturity corresponded so well to the themes of early Irish spirituality, carved on the original celtic scripture crosses.

Just as in the scripture crosses, in the map of faith maturity Jesus is central, present in power, saving, healing, forgiving, freeing us into faith and hope. And around Christ are

Faith Community
(not a private
spirituality)

Prayer

1. Liturgy (Mass and the Sacraments)
2. Personal prayer.
3. Prayer with one another (family prayer, shared prayer). Prayer transforming us.

The Map of Faith Maturity

Commitment

1. To the people of the community.
2. To the concerns of the community, the Church, the world and the poor.
3. Expressed by giving
   – time,
   – energy,
   – priority.

Conversion

1. To the person of Jesus Christ, the Son of the living God.
2. To the presence of Christ: Eucharist, an active presence; where 2 or 3 are gathered. Every human person is sacred, and all creation: we're always walking on holy ground.
3. To the power of Christ, to heal, to teach, to forgive, to set free, to save. Jesus is the only one who can save. It is his power we rely on.
4. To the mission of Jesus: to the ends of the earth; to every human person; to transform the world in which we live.

Cross of words:
Map of Faith Maturity

gathered his faithful people, in unity, in *muintearas* – communion – praying in the liturgical assembly and in the family, and understanding the needs of people around them, in the parish, in the local community, in the diocese, in the worldwide Church and in the world at large. The great Irish crosses are not just a decoration in our landscape, but are themselves a kind of map of faith maturity, landmarks for a journey, for the pilgrimage of life.

The closer we get to the great Irish scripture crosses, the more contemporary they seem. Their spirituality reflects the spirituality of their age, but it is a spirituality which we have reclaimed since Vatican II. It is a spirituality which was expressed in the Eucharistic Congress in Dublin in June 2012. It is a communal spirituality, a church spirituality. It is earthy and heavenly. There is a treatise, in Old Irish, on the Mass in the Stowe Missal, written in the great monastery of St Maelruáin in Tallaght in the Dublin mountains in the year AD 800. It describes the Mass as the meeting place of the heavenly and earthly Church. Our people in the early Irish Church understood that when they gathered to offer the Mass they were in the company of the angels and saints, and of Mary, mother of the heavenly and earthly Church. There is the same sense of heavenly realities touching the physical realities of our lives in this 'Blessing of the Senses', or the Blessing of St Fursa, from the seventh century:

In Irish:

Go raibh cuing reachta Dé ar an ngualainn seo;
Go raibh fiosrú an Spioraid Naoimh ar an gceann seo;
Go raibh comhartha Chríost san éadan seo;
Go raibh éisteacht an Spioraid Naoimh sna cluasa seo;
Go raibh boltanú an Spioraid Naoimh sa tsrón seo;
Go raibh amharc mhuintir neimhe sna súile seo;
Go raibh comhrá mhuintir neimhe sa bhéal seo;
Go raibh obair eaglais Dé sna lámha seo;
Go raibh leas Dé agus na gcomharsan sna cosa seo.
Gurab áit do Dhia an croí seo,
Agus gura le Dia, Athair uile, an duine seo.
Amen.

Adapted into English:

May the yoke of God's commandments be upon your shoulder;
May the visitation of the Holy Spirit be upon your head;
May the sign of Christ be on your forehead;
May the listening of the Holy Spirit be in your ears;
May the fragrance of the Holy Spirit be in your nose;
May the vision of the people of heaven be in your eyes;
May the conversation of the people of heaven be in your mouth;
May the work of God's church be in your hands;
May the good of God and the neighbours be in your feet.
May your heart be a place for God,
And may this person belong to God, the Father of all.
Amen.

The faith community of the early Irish Church had a deep sense of the bond that existed between them as a community, as a united family, but they were also aware of the presence of Jesus in them and among them. As Chiara Lubich, the foundress of the Focolare Movement, said: 'Jesus among us makes Jesus within us grow.' St Paul talked of 'the mystery that has been hidden throughout the ages and generations but has now been revealed to his saints. To them God chose to make known how great among the nations are the riches of the glory of this mystery, which is Christ in you, the hope of glory'. (*Col 1:26–27*) *Jesus among us, the hope of our glory* – that is the mystery of the Church, and the meaning and mystery of the great crosses of Ireland.

Maps

Locations of Great Irish Crosses

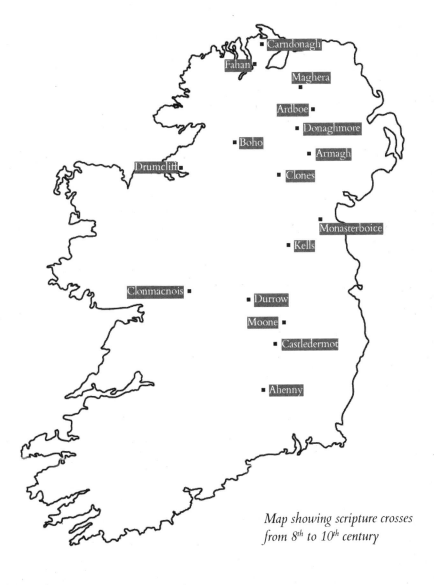

*Map showing scripture crosses
from 8th to 10th century*

*12th century crosses in
Connaught and Munster*

Bibliography

Françoise Henry:
I   *Irish Art in the Early Christian Period.*
     Methuen and Cornell University Press, 1965.
II   *Irish Art during the Viking Invasions.*
     Methuen and Cornell University Press, 1967.
III *Irish Art in the Romanesque Period.*
     Methuen and Cornell University Press, 1970.

Helen M. Roe:
    The High Crosses of Kells.
    Meath Archaeological and Historical Society, 1966.

Peter Harbison:
    Irish High Crosses, with the figure sculptures explained.
    The Boyne Valley Honey Company, 1994, reprinted 2001.

Roger Stalley:
    Irish High Crosses.
    Trinity College, Dublin, 1996.

Hilary Richardson:
    Preface to *Studies in Early Christian and Medieval Irish Art.*
    (Françoise Henry) London, 1985.

Domhnall Ó Murchadha:
    'Stone Sculpture in Pre-Norman Ireland.'
    The Capuchin Annual, Dublin, 1969.

The Boho Cross, Co. Fermanagh

Seán Ó Duinn OSB:
> *The Rites of Brigid, Goddess and Saint.*
> Columba Press, Dublin, 2005.

A.T. Lucas:
> *Penal Crucifixes.*
> Co. Louth Archaeological Society, 1954,
> Dublin, The Stationery Office, 1958.

Michael Mullins:
> *Commentaries on the Gospels of Matthew, Mark, Luke and John.*
> Columba Press, Dublin, 2007, 2005, 2010, 2003.

Donald Senior CP:
> *The Passion of Jesus in the Gospel of Mark, Matthew, Luke and John.*
> Michael Glazier, Wilmington, Delaware, 1984, 1985, 1989, 1991.
> (Available from Liturgical Press, Collegeville, Minnesota.)

Raymond E. Brown:
> *The Epistles of John.*
> Doubleday and Company Inc., 1982.

Jennifer O'Reilly:
> *The Book of Kells, Folio 114.*
> Article in 'Treasures of Irish Christianity', Veritas 2012.

John R. Walsh:
> *Noble Story: A short history of the diocese of Derry.*
> Editions du Signe, 2001.

An tAthair Donnchadh Ó Floinn:
> *Dúchas agus Creideamh in Éirinn,*
> 'More than a Language.'
> Cumann na Sagart, 2006.

National Museum of Ireland:
> Irish High Crosses Exhibition,
> Catalogue.